INTERNATIONAL LAW AND
THE USES OF OUTER SPACE

THE MELLAND SCHILL LECTURES

delivered at the University of Manchester and published by the University Press

The Law of International Institutions in Europe
by A. H. Robertson, B.C.L., S.J.D., 1961

The Role of International Law in the Elimination of War
by Professor Quincy Wright, 1961

The Acquisition of Territory in International Law
by Professor R. Y. Jennings, 1962

The Sources and Evidences of International Law
by Clive Parry, LL.D., 1965

Rights in Air Space
by D. H. N. Johnson, M.A., LL.B., 1965

International Law and the Practitioner
by Sir Francis A. Vallat, K.C.M.G., Q.C., 1966

The Law of the Sea
by D. W. Bowett, M.A., LL.B., Ph.D., 1967

Modern Diplomatic Law
by M. Hardy, M.A., LL.M., 1968

International Law and the Uses of Outer Space
by J. E. S. Fawcett, M.A.

OTHER BOOKS IN INTERNATIONAL LAW

Self-Defence in International Law
by D. W. Bowett, M.A., LL.B., Ph.D.

Human Rights in Europe
by A. H. Robertson, B.C.L., S.J.D.

The Legal Problems of Foreign Investment in Developing Countries
by E. I. Nwogugu, LL.B., Ph.D.

The Settlement of Boundary Disputes in International Law
by A. O. Cukwurah, LL.B., Ph.D.

Human Rights in National and International Law
edited by A. H. Robertson, B.C.L., S.J.D.

Legal Aspects of Foreign Investment in the European Economic Community
by W. H. Balekjian, Dr. rer. pol., Dr. Jur., Ph.D.

INTERNATIONAL LAW AND THE USES OF OUTER SPACE

by

J. E. S. FAWCETT, M.A.

Fellow of All Souls College, Oxford

MANCHESTER UNIVERSITY PRESS

U.S.A.: OCEANA PUBLICATIONS INC.

Published by the University of Manchester at
The University Press
316–324 Oxford Road, Manchester 13

U.S.A.
Oceana Publications Inc.
75 Main Street, Dobbs Ferry, N.Y. 10522

distributed in India by
N. M. Tripathi Private Limited
Princess Street, Bombay-2

Library of Congress Catalog Card Number 68–17736

G.B. SBN: 7190 0320 2

Oceana Book No. 23-9

Printed in Great Britain by Butler & Tanner Ltd., Frome and London

FOREWORD

BY her Will, the late Miss Olive Schill of Prestbury, Cheshire, an old friend of the University, whose portrait is painted in Lady Katharine Chorley's *Manchester Made Them*, left the sum of £10,000 to the University in memory of her brother, Melland Schill, who died in the 1914–18 war. The annual income from this sum is to be used to promote and publish a series of public lectures of the highest possible standard dealing with International Law.

Mr Fawcett has had a distinguished career in the Foreign Office, at the International Monetary Fund, and is now a member of the European Commission of Human Rights at the Council of Europe in Strasbourg. He is Fellow of All Souls College, Oxford, and is the author of numerous articles and works on international law and allied subjects. In addition, he possesses the unusual advantage of being a keen and practising member of the British Astronomical Association, an interest shared by very few lawyers and of vital import in the present lectures.

Manchester's reputation in the sphere of astronomy is well known, and it is hoped that these lectures will appeal not only to students of law and politics, but also to many scientists in the universities, as well as to the general reader.

B. A. WORTLEY

Faculty of Law
Manchester University

CONTENTS

Chapter I

RESOLUTION AND TREATY

THE uses of outer space have come in a bare decade to be governed by a number of rules of law. In this they are not alone. The continental shelf, the legal personality of international organizations, and the international protection of human rights, have all exhibited in very different fields the same kind of rapid legal evolution. The special factors that are at work in this acceleration of international law in the uses of outer space are the reduction of the scale of the earth and its neighbourhood which these uses have themselves brought about; a vast expansion of scientific research, engineering techniques, industrial capacity and military ambitions; and the multiplier effects of all these factors operating together. Overriding all is the need that the uses of outer space shall be for peace not war. Space law then is a most fitting topic for these lectures, founded as they are for advancement of the knowledge of international law and in memory of Melland Schill who gave his life in the first World War.

Just as space itself is a continuum from the surface of the earth outwards, so the uses of outer space are an integral part, in their infrastructure, direction and effects, of contemporary life. When a great rocket carries a spacecraft into outer space it represents a huge expenditure of money and of the labour and skill of thousands of people around the world, who have come to depend for their livelihood upon it. The direction and purposes of this effort raise large political issues of the right use of public money, of choices between public and private enterprise, and of the proper places in society of scientific research and of military objectives. To estimate its effects is still too early; we are, for example, only beginning to see the educational potentialities of communications satellites, the far-ranging consequences for agriculture of accurate global weather forecasting, and the possibility that the uses of outer space may, by some unforeseen twist, do irreversible damage in the atmosphere or on the ground. Outer space is far closer to us now than Antarctica.

In space law, as elsewhere, we must have some agreement about the meaning of the terms we are using. Descriptions of outer space vary. Sometimes it comprises the orbital paths of earth satellites and beyond;[1] or it is considered as lying beyond the atmosphere of the earth;[2] or it may be referred to as including,[3] or as being distinct from, the celestial bodies.[4] No definition has yet been agreed, and this raises issues of State sovereignty, which must be discussed later. In these lectures 'outer space' will be taken to describe that part of space where spacecraft do their essential work.

Spacecraft may be used as a general term to describe any object, whether it is a vehicle or not, which goes into Earth orbit or beyond, but we can distinguish functionally among spacecraft between satellites, which go into orbit around the Earth; space probes, which escape from the Earth and either go into orbit around a celestial body or, after completing their mission, into orbit around the Sun; space platforms, which are satellites of the Earth or a celestial body, serving as a base or auxiliary for operations of other spacecraft; orbiting observations; and spacecraft, soft-landed on a celestial body, which may be called a station, whether unmanned or manned.

On this approach machines, of which the American X-15 is the archetype, are not spacecraft. In what conditions they are to be regarded as, or as not, aircraft depends on their mode of flight. If they develop the capacity to leave the ground as an aircraft and go into Earth orbit as a satellite, the same functional test of the mode of flight must be applied.[5]

Lastly, the launchers of spacecraft must not be forgotten for, though they may fall rapidly away after the flight has begun, they

[1] General Assembly Resolution 1721B–XVI, para. 1. The International Telecommunications Union Radio Regulations define 'deep space' as space beyond the orbit of the Moon.

[2] ITU Radio Regulations, Reg. 84AE defines a 'space station' as 'a station located on an object which is beyond, is intended to go beyond, or has been beyond the major portion of the Earth's atmosphere'; Nuclear Test Ban Treaty, Article I, 'prohibits tests (*a*) in the atmosphere; beyond its limits, including outer space'. Compare the French term for 'outer space', 'l'espace extra-atmosphèrique'.

[3] Outer Space Treaty, Article 1 and also in title: 'outer space, including the Moon and other celestial bodies'.

[4] Resolutions 1721A–XVI, para. 1(*b*); 1962–XVIII, para. 2: 'outer space and celestial bodies'.

[5] For similar reasoning see *Polpen Shipping Co. v. Commercial Union Assurance Co.* [1942] 74 *Lloyds List Rep.*, 157 (a 'flying boat' is not a 'ship or vessel' since its 'real work is to fly').

may go into orbit or beyond before separation from the spacecraft and add, temporarily at least, to the hardware drifting in outer space.

The Ad Hoc Committee on the Peaceful Uses of Outer Space, reporting to the General Assembly in 1959, recommended certain legal problems in outer space for priority consideration; the free and common exploration and use of outer space; liability for injury or damage caused by spacecraft; the allocation of radio frequencies in space communications; and the registration, tracking and re-entry of spacecraft. The Committee did not consider as matters of urgency the determination of the lower limits of outer space; the protection of public health and safety; the exploration and settlement of celestial bodies; or the mutual interference of spacecraft. Developments since 1959, and particularly the General Assembly Resolutions and the Outer Space Treaty, prompt a different selection of problems for discussion here. I propose to consider in turn the effects in international law of the Resolutions and the Treaty; the character and limits of State jurisdiction and control over spacecraft; the military uses of outer space and the celestial bodies; the management of space operations and control of their side-effects, including responsibility for damage; and the use and regulation of space communications.

That the exploration and uses of outer space and the celestial bodies are governed by the provisions of the United Nations Charter is both clear and necessary. The applicability of the material provisions of the Charter is in no case expressly limited *ratione loci*: in particular, Article 2(4) does not in any way localize the use or threat of force, even though the political independence or territorial integrity of a State must be the object. Further, the fact that the uses of outer space are, in their form and their purpose, closely integrated with multifarious human activities on the earth makes their relative remoteness irrelevant. Indeed, it is not correct to speak of the *extension* of the Charter to outer space; the uses of outer space fall inexorably within it. The question as to what sectors, if any, of the uses of outer space can be said to fall essentially within the domestic jurisdiction of a State, will be considered later in the context of claims of jurisdiction.

It is within the framework of the United Nations Charter that the

General Assembly Resolutions on outer space and the Outer Space Treaty have evolved; and Article 3 of the Treaty provides that:

States parties to the Treaty shall carry on activities in the exploration and use of outer space, including the Moon and other celestial bodies, in accordance with international law, including the Charter of the United Nations . . .

General Assembly Resolution 1962–XVIII was the culmination of long debates, much negotiation, and a series of resolutions extending over a number of years. In 1958, the General Assembly, prompted by the co-operative success of the International Geophysical Year, established by Resolution 1348–XIII, a Committee on the Peaceful Uses of Outer Space, to report on the activities and resources of the U.N. and its specialized agencies that could be devoted to organized co-operation in the peaceful uses of outer space, and on the legal problems arising out of 'programmes to explore outer space'. In the following year the Committee was made permanent by Resolution 1472–XIV, with similar terms of reference. From 1961 to 1963, five further Resolutions were adopted. Their contents may be divided into recommendations against dangerous activities in outer space; technical recommendations addressed to the Committee on the Peaceful Uses of Outer Space, the World Meteorological Organization, and the International Telecommunications Union: and declarations of general legal principles applicable to the uses of outer space. Notable in these Resolutions is the stress laid upon the common interest of all countries in the right uses of outer space, regardless of their economic or scientific development, and upon the essential role of the 'international scientific community', an expression which appears in Resolution 1472–XIV and is taken up in the Outer Space Treaty.

* * *

Let us turn now to the 'Declaration of legal principles governing the activities of States in the exploration and use of outer space', which is the full title of Resolution 1962–XVIII. The Declaration made its first appearance in December 1961[1] when the General Assembly 'commended' to States 'for their guidance' the principles that

(*a*) International law, including the Charter of the United Nations, applies to outer space and celestial bodies.

[1] Resolution 1721A–XVI (20.12.1961).

(*b*) Outer space and celestial bodies are free for exploration and use by all States in conformity with international law and are not subject to national appropriation.

Resolution 1962–XVIII, adopted unanimously, like the earlier Resolution, goes further in that it is expressed to be declaratory of legal principles, and extends their applicability. It declares six principles of law as governing the uses of outer space: equality; common use; State responsibility; corporate responsibility; ownership and control; and common humanity.

Equality of States in their exploration and use of outer space reflects their equality under Article 2(1) of the U.N. Charter, and like it, is an equality in law not in fact. States have equal rights of access to and use of outer space, but the principle does not assure to them equally the economic resources and technological means of exercising those rights, or the benefits to be derived from them.

Common use precludes appropriation. Further, the rule that neither outer space nor the celestial bodies may be appropriated by a State, 'by claim of sovereignty, by means of use or occupation, or otherwise', would preserve them from that appropriation, even with the acquiescence of other States, from which another great area of *res communis*, the high seas, is not immune.[1]

The rule of State responsibility is declared applicable to outer space activities in a number of ways, some of which are in a degree novel. Apart from the normal responsibility of a State for acts or omissions of its governmental agencies, a State is declared responsible for outer space activities carried on by national but non-governmental bodies, or by an international organization of which it is a member.[2] Further, in addition to tortious liability for damage caused by a spacecraft or its component parts,[3] the concepts of nuisance and

[1] Territorial Sea Convention, Article 5(2).

[2] '5. States bear international responsibility for national activities in outer space, whether carried on by governmental agencies or by non-governmental entities, and for assuring that national activities are carried on in conformity with the principles set forth in the present Declaration. The activities of non-governmental entities in outer space shall require authorization and continuing supervision by the State concerned. When activities are carried on in outer space by an international organization, responsibility for compliance with the principles set forth in this Declaration shall be borne by the international organization and by the States participating in it.'

[3] '8. Each State which launches or procures the launching of an object into outer space, and each State from whose territory or facility an object is launched,

abuse of rights are introduced, to be further developed in the Outer Space Treaty, to check potential harmful interference with other uses of outer space.[1]

The rule of corporate responsibility is a corollary of the right of an international organization to bring an international claim in respect of loss or damage incurred by it in the performance of its legitimate functions.[2]

The principle of continuing ownership and control of spacecraft, after they have left the ground[3] has a number of elements: first, it disposes of the idea that by the act of launching a spacecraft, which is not designed to make a controlled return to the earth, ownership in it is abandoned and that it becomes *res derelicta*. Secondly, jurisdiction and control of spacecraft, whether manned or unmanned, is to rest, on the analogy of ships and aircraft, upon national registration in a particular State. Thirdly, ownership is distinguished from jurisdiction and control and is not confined to the State or its agencies.

The principle of common humanity is given a limited application in the assistance to be afforded to astronauts in distress, which is extended in the Outer Space Treaty.

That the uses of outer space be peaceful in the sense that they shall not involve the unlawful use of force is a seventh principle underlying

---

is internationally liable for damage to a foreign State or to its natural or juridical persons by such object or its component parts on the Earth, in air space, or in outer space.'

[1] '6. In the exploration and use of outer space, States shall be guided by the principle of co-operation and mutual assistance, and shall conduct all their activities in outer space with due regard for the corresponding interests of other States. If a State has reason to believe that an outer space activity or experiment planned by it or its nationals would cause potentially harmful interference with activities of other States in the peaceful exploration and use of outer space, it shall undertake appropriate international consultations before proceeding with any such activity or experiment. A State which has reason to believe that an outer space activity or experiment planned by another State would cause potentially harmful interference with activities in the peaceful exploration and use of outer space may request consultation concerning the activity or experiment.'

[2] Compare *Reparation for Injuries Case* [1949] *ICJ Rep.* at 179 (the U.N. held to be 'capable of possessing international rights and *duties*').

[3] '7. The State on whose registry an object launched into outer space is carried shall retain jurisdiction and control over such object, and any personnel, thereon while in outer space. Ownership of objects launched into outer space, and of their component parts, is not affected by their passage through outer space or by their return to the Earth. Such objects or component parts found beyond the limits of the state of registry shall be returned to that State, which shall furnish identifying data upon request prior to return.'

all the Resolutions and the Outer Space Treaty. It rests on the United Nations Charter, in particular Articles 2(3) and 2(4), but is not one of the declared legal principles. The Resolutions in fact go no further than to give it two particular applications: the condemnation of propaganda designed or likely to provoke or encourage any threat to the peace, breach of the peace, or act of aggression, is extended to activities in outer space;[1] and States are called on

(*a*) to refrain from placing in orbit around the Earth any objects carrying nuclear weapons or any other kinds of weapons of mass destruction, installing such weapons on celestial bodies, or stationing such weapons in outer space in any other manner;

(*b*) to refrain from causing, encouraging or in any way participating in the conduct of the foregoing activities.[2]

The immediate question to be asked is, what is the character and effect of this declaration of legal principles?

It is plain that we have to do here not with an ordinary recommendation by the General Assembly, addressed to one or more States under Articles 10–14 of the Charter, but a declaration of the same order, though perhaps of a lower degree, as the Declarations of 1948, 1960 and 1965 on human rights and self-determination and racial discrimination.

The Declaration on outer space has two further significant features: it was adopted unanimously, a consummation rare among General Assembly Resolutions, and it was expressly entitled a 'declaration of legal principles'. Lord McNair has said of such international declarations that, while it is unsafe to generalize upon them, there is no reason of principle why they should not establish obligations. It is submitted that it would not be unsafe to say that an international declaration would establish rules of law, if the following four conditions at least are satisfied: that the sponsoring States have authority to make the declaration: that the declaration serves a common interest; that the principles declared are capable of functioning as rules of law without further elaboration; and that the sponsoring States intend to observe them as such.

That States may in combination have authority to declare principles or rules of international law is an observed fact, of which the

[1] Resolution 110–II (3.11.1947), a 'cold war' formula, cited rather disconnectedly in the preamble to Resolution 1962–XVIII.

[2] Resolution 1884–XVIII (17.10.1963).

Suez Canal Convention 1888 is a signal example, but it is a political fact and its explanation lies outside the law. So the International Court observed that

> fifty States, [then] representing the vast majority of the members of the international community, had the power, in conformity with international law, to bring into being an entity possessing objective international personality, and not merely personality recognized by them alone, together with capacity to bring international claims.[1]

If 'power' is understood here in the sense of legal authorization, the whole proposition of course becomes circular; but it means rather that political authority, which States are recognized as having, to take certain kinds of action in combination. The kinds of action, and its effectiveness, are limited by what other States, or the peoples of the world, are prepared politically to accept. The authority of States acting together through the medium of a General Assembly Resolution is to be understood in the same way. The International Court stressed that the establishment of the United Nations was the work of the vast majority of the members of the international community; where a resolution or declaration is adopted by those members unanimously, the fact of authority is still more manifest.

That there is a common interest of the whole world in the present and potential uses of outer space, which the declaration seeks to govern, hardly needs demonstration, and so the General Assembly

> . . . *Recognizing* the common interest of all mankind in the progress of the exploration and use of outer space for peaceful purposes, . . .
>
> *Solemnly declares* that . . . 1. The exploration and use of outer space shall be carried on for the benefit and in the interest of all mankind.[2]

The third and fourth conditions are more critical. Are the declared principles rules of law, which the sponsoring States intend to observe as such, or are they standards or directive principles only?[3] There is formidable authority in the highest places that they are the latter. In 1964 the delegate of the Soviet Union in the Legal Subcommittee[4]

[1] *Reparation for Injuries Case* [1949] *ICJ Rep*. at 185.

[2] Resolution 1962–XVIII. For the concept of 'solidarity' as a ground for the creation of international obligations see *de Rothschild v. Teuscher* [1953] *Belgium, Trib. Civ. de Bruxelles* 20 *ILR* 655, 659 (interpreting the Interallied Declaration on Acts of Dispossession, London: January 1943).

[3] For an example of directive principles see *Constitution of India*, Article 39; they are not enforceable in the courts but are 'fundamental in the governance of the country and it shall be the duty of the State to apply these provisions in making laws', Article 37.

[4] Of the U.N. Committee on the Peaceful Uses of Outer Space.

'regretted . . . that the Declaration was in the form of a General Assembly resolution which laid no obligations on the Governments of States Members of the United Nations' and called for a treaty or international agreement 'whose provisions would be binding on all parties'. Similarly the representative of France observed that 'the resolutions which had been adopted' could not give rise to legal obligations for Member States; they had no binding force and were no more than 'declarations of intention'. To the Hungarian representative the declared principles were 'only a recommendation and therefore not binding' and for the Italian they 'lacked the force of an international instrument'. These observations are made from a formal approach, in which the declaration of principles is seen as a General Assembly Resolution, not differing essentially from other Resolutions, and being therefore hortatory only, or at most a declaration of intentions.

In the Resolution, specifically directed to Resolution 1962–XVIII and adopted by the International Law Association, a non-governmental body, at the Tokyo Conference in 1964, the Conference

Welcoming this further action by the General Assembly to develop a legal regime for outer space;

Noting that this Declaration states legal principles accepted by the Members of the United Nations;

Urges that States engaging in activities in outer space shall seek actively to conform their conduct to the principles contained in the Declaration.

The 'noting' clause is adroitly ambiguous. It could be read as holding that the members of the U.N. had already, and before the declaration, accepted the legal principles as rules of law; or that they had accepted them as directive principles; or that they accepted them as one or the other by virtue of the declaration itself; or the clause may be no more than a record of the obvious fact that the members accepted the declaration in voting for it.

Support could be found for this formal approach in the Declaration of Paris 1856, commonly invoked as the archetype of international law-making instruments. Its outline is worth recalling:

The Plenipotentiaries . . .

Considering:

That maritime law, in time of war, has long been the subject of deplorable dispute . . .

That it is consequently advantageous to establish uniformity of doctrine on a point of so much importance;

That the Plenipotentiaries, assembled at the Congress of Paris, could not better respond to the intentions by which their Governments are animated than by trying to introduce into international relations fixed principles in this respect . . .

The four rules follow, on privateering; neutral flag; neutral goods; and blockade. States not represented at the Congress are invited to accede to the Declaration, which however

is not and shall not be obligatory except between those Powers who have acceded or shall accede to it.

The Declaration of Paris and Resolution 1962–XVIII have marked similarities in their subject-matter, their purpose, and the circumstances of their adoption. They are both concerned with global problems, the freedom of the seas and the freedom of outer space; both seek to establish fixed principles or rules of law, where hitherto the law has been uncertain or missing; and the last paragraph quoted from the preamble to the Declaration of Paris would with change of title be apt to describe the adoption of the Resolution by the General Assembly. But the law-making character of the Declaration of Paris is given without equivocation a strictly contractual basis: only States that sign or accede assume the rights and obligations to be derived from the rules declared; and the recent law-making Conventions on the Law of the Sea and on Diplomatic and Consular Relations are constructed on a similar pattern. On the other hand the United States did not ratify but always accepted in practice the Declaration of Paris; and the Hague Convention IV–1907, known as the Hague Regulations, has long been recognized, and in particular by the Nuremberg Tribunal, as embodying customary law, notwithstanding the contractual participation clause in it.

This conflict between the contractual form and law-making function of an international convention is sometimes said to be resolved by regarding the provisions of the convention as evidence of customary law, or as a source of law, or more subtly as a potential source of law. This approach has been made to the principles declared in Resolution 1962–XVIII; so a representative on the Legal Subcommittee said:

. . . that a Declaration of legal principles by the General Assembly, especially if universally adopted and adhered to in practice, may be valuable evidence of international custom, which in turn is an important source of law.

Without following all the involutions of this Delphic utterance, we may ask whether Resolution 1962–XVIII is evidence of international custom. Are the legal principles there declared

> in accordance with a constant and uniform usage practised by the States in question.[1]

This formulation of the test by the International Court emphasizes that such usage need not be universal, but is sufficient if it is common to the States generally involved in the situations in which the practice is to be found. We might also ask whether the declared legal principles reflect a consciousness of established duties such as that invoked by the Permanent Court:[2]

> . . . only if such abstention [of States from instituting criminal proceedings in exercise of extraterritorial jurisdiction] were based on their being conscious of a duty to abstain would it be possible to speak of an international custom.

But, even granted that customary rules of international law may, when it is necessary, be established rapidly, it would be difficult to found new rules for outer space on the practice only of the two principal space-users in the few years between 1957 and the adoption of the Resolution, for there were other space-users which could not be said to be yet committed to any particular practice, if only by reason of the limited extent of their operations. Further, none of the declared principles, not already embodied in the United Nations Charter, had yet had in 1963 such application in practice as to found an *opinio juris*; and indeed some operations such as the West Ford experiment with orbiting dipoles—the 'copper needles'—or the Starfish operation involving high-altitude nuclear explosions, were doubtfully consistent with them. On the one point at which practice may, as has been argued, have created customary rights—the overflight by satellites of foreign territory—Resolution 1962–XVIII is silent. The notion of customary international law is not then of great help in understanding the Resolution.

A test of our third condition which suggests itself, of whether the Resolution sets out rules of law or directive principles only, is to ask

[1] *The Asylum Case* [1950] *ICJ Rep.* at 276–7 *per curiam.*
[2] *The Lotus Case* [1927] *PCIJ: Ser. A 10* at 28.

whether the declared principles are self-executing. In borrowing this notion from the different context of incorporation of treaties in municipal law, we must modify it and say that the declared principles in Resolution 1962–XVIII could be regarded as self-executing, on two conditions; if they are reasonably precise, and if they do not on the face of them call for further steps by States to transform them into rules of international law. The principles of free and common use of outer space, international responsibility, ownership and control, and common humanity, do not obviously fail to satisfy the first of these conditions, even though the expression 'outer space' is itself left undefined. It would, as we shall later see, be difficult to deny that spacecraft in orbit or beyond are in 'outer space', for the purpose of the declared principles as well as in the general usage that has now grown up. The fact that the lower limit of outer space towards the Earth is not determined would not invalidate the declared principles as a whole, any more than the variable widths of the territorial sea, and the existence of a 'contiguous zone' jurisdiction, invalidate the rules governing the use of the high seas.

However, in considering whether the declared principles call for further steps by States to transform them into rules of international law, we have to take General Assembly Resolution 1963–XVIII into account. In this the General Assembly

> 1. *Recommends* that consideration should be given to incorporating in international agreement form, in the future as appropriate, legal principles governing the activities of States in the exploration and use of outer space;
> 2. *Requests* the Committee on the Peaceful Uses of Outer Space to continue to study and report on legal problems which may arise in the exploration and use of outer space, and in particular to arrange for the prompt preparation of draft international agreements on liability for damage caused by objects launched into outer space and on assistance to return of astronauts and space vehicles;
> 3. *Further requests* the Committee . . . to report to the General Assembly at its nineteenth session on the results achieved in preparing these two agreements.

What is astonishing about these paragraphs is that they are drafted as though Resolution 1962–XVIII did not exist. The lack of any cross-reference between two obviously linked Resolutions, adopted on the same day, makes interpretation at least of the first paragraph of the second Resolution uncertain. It must be supposed that 'legal principles' in the first paragraph must include the legal principles declared in Resolution 1962–XVIII; on the other hand the words 'in the future as appropriate' suggest that the drafters of the paragraph did not consider that the embodiment of all the declared principles in treaty form was necessary to their effectiveness, though the selection of two of the declared principles as subject-matter for special international agreements, implies that at least those were not thought capable of being implemented as they stand.

But even if some of the declared principles could be implemented directly as rules of law, we cannot say that the Resolution as a whole satisfies our last condition that the sponsoring States intended to observe its provisions as rules of law; for, despite the unanimous adoption of the declared principles and the protestations of support for them, the fact is that international legislation here, as in other fields, is still rooted in the treaty process. States and their peoples may subscribe to, support and even intend to observe, certain legal principles, but they do not feel themselves bound to do so, unless these principles are enclosed in the felt security of a treaty.

If then we survey the record of the General Assembly we can see that Article 13(1) of the Charter is being implemented through two processes. The first is the preparation of drafts by the International Law Commission, their close examination by governments both outside and in the General Assembly, their adoption by the General Assembly for reference to a specially convoked international conference, and their final transformation into a law-making convention. The second process is, in comparison with the first, unorganized, imprecise and often inconclusive, though it is sometimes completed by a treaty. It is represented by a series of General Assembly Resolutions, of which Resolution 1962–XVIII is one, and which may still fairly claim to have furthered 'the progressive development of international law' called for by Article 13(1), in that they have formulated general principles of law or international conduct,[1] or authoritatively interpreted the United Nations Charter, sometimes by

[1] Resolution 95–I (Nuremberg Charter principles) (11.12.1946); Universal Declaration of Human Rights (6.12.1948); Resolution 1653–XVI (Prohibition of Use of Nuclear Weapons) (24.11.1961); Resolution 1803–XVII (Permanent Sovereignty over Natural Resources); Resolution 1904–XVIII (Racial Discrimination) (20.11.1963). See Statute of the International Law Commission, Article 15, describing the field for progressive development as 'subjects which have not yet been regulated by international law or in regard to which the law has not yet been sufficiently developed in the practice of States'.

important extension.[1] But we must wait on the future to see whether the requirement of the consent of States in international law-making can ever become independent of the treaty process and be satisfied by a vote in the General Assembly or an international conference convened by it. In the Law of the Sea Conventions at least, the treaty form has already begun to seem like a grumbling appendix.

However for the present the treaty process must continue to serve. But, if a General Assembly Resolution, even though cast in the solemn form of a declaration of legal principles, does not create rules of law, a treaty has the inherent limitation that it can only create rules between the contracting parties: neither is legislation in the full sense. Yet each complements the other; and where we have a treaty, preceded by a General Assembly Resolution laying down general principles, we look to the treaty as the legal means of their practical implementation. If this is to be achieved, we should require of the treaty three things as a minimum: that it makes express and precise those international rights and obligations, which are only implied or indicated in general terms in the Resolution; that it provides means of securing their observance; and that, since its provisions are to function as rules of international law, it must be durable. If the treaty fails to meet these requirements, it can add little to the strength of a Resolution, and may even weaken it.

* * *

The Outer Space Treaty was concluded in December 1966 within the United Nations. It is in large part composed of passages from General Assembly Resolutions, and in particular Resolution 1962–XVIII, adapted with little or no change. However there are some new elements. The principle that the uses of outer space must be peaceful in manner and in purpose is asserted and extended in provisions for partial demilitarization of outer space and the celestial bodies; there are arrangements for co-operation in the tracking of spacecraft in flight, for the inspection of spacecraft and spacestations on the Moon and other celestial bodies, and for the avoidance of contamination.

[1] e.g. Resolution 1514–XV (Granting of Independence to Colonial Countries and Peoples) (14.12.1960); Resolution 614–V(Criteria of Self-government). Of the former Resolution Dr Clive Parry in his Melland Schill Lectures has said: 'Can even the nine abstaining members deny that the law of territorial sovereignty has been, or must be rewritten, as a result of that Resolution?'

But the Treaty, by bare repetition of paragraphs of Resolutions 1884–XVIII and 1962–XVIII, does not elucidate them or make them more precise, and its few provisions that are new are so loosely drafted as to suggest that the authors did not expect them to be put to a real test of interpretation, but thought that as long as the instrument looked reasonably like a treaty, the main purpose was served; and this purpose is not perhaps far to seek. For in their mutual search for a continuing *détente*, in face of great obstacles, the Governments of the United States and the Soviet Union, the principal space-users, must have seen an admirable opportunity in the uses of outer space. The General Assembly Resolutions, for which they had voted, provided a ready framework; and a general treaty, to which they might lead the United Nations, would have the psychological impact in all countries of international undertakings given and received, and be seen as a comforting measure of international co-operation. But, we may suppose, this reasonable objective was seen to be restricted on the one hand by the need, if the treaty was to be easily concluded, to avoid controversy over the scope and meaning of the declared legal principles on outer space, and on the other by a desire to avoid too open commitments in this strange new region. The main purpose then was to have a treaty, but to give it the smallest possible force and effect beyond the General Assembly Resolutions.

So no provision is made for the authoritative interpretation of the Treaty or for the settlement of disputes over its application. No sanction appears for non-observance of its provisions, nor is there any indication of what action States may take to counter harmful effects of the uses of outer space, with which a number of Articles are concerned. It may be that some use will be made of amendment machinery, but the provisions for amendment are strictly contractual and an amendment is to be operative only for States accepting it after it has been accepted by a majority of contracting States. Finally, after the Treaty has been in force for a year, any contracting State may withdraw from it on the sole condition of giving one year's notice and without even the modest restraint upon withdrawal to be found in the Nuclear Test Ban Treaty. Here the Law of the Sea Conventions stand in sharp contrast.

In the Outer Space Treaty we have then a rigidly contractual instrument, in essence a bilateral arrangement between the principal space-users. Apart from its provisions for partial demilitarization of outer space, tracking and inspection, it does little or nothing to elaborate or secure the principles already set out in General Assembly Resolutions. It may even be that this ill-constructed and precarious instrument is a retrograde step. For in the wise words of Dr Jenks, written before the conclusion of the Outer Space Treaty:[1]

> The authority of the Declaration of Legal Principles may be expected to grow with the passage of years. While it is somewhat less than a treaty it must already be regarded as rather more than a statement of custom.

Though Resolution 1962–XVIII is for the most part a declaration, not of rules of international law, but of directive principles, it may like other similar General Assembly Resolutions, be regarded as forming part of an international *ordre public*, to which States should strive to make their policies conform. So an Italian court, in one of the most remarkable judicial decisions on international law of recent years, did not hesitate to test the Iranian oil industry legislation for its consistency with the General Assembly Resolution (1803–XVII) on Permanent Sovereignty over Natural Resources.[2]

The conclusion of a weak treaty may serve only to frustrate this development.

[1] C. W. Jenks, *Space Law* (Stevens, 1965), 185.
[2] *Anglo-Iranian Oil Co. v. S.U.P.O.R.* [1955] *ILR* 40.

Chapter II

JURISDICTION

WHATEVER may be the relationship, and respective forms, of the General Assembly Resolutions and the Outer Space Treaty, at least two principles can be found in them, which must be regarded as satisfying our four conditions for being rules of law. Formulated in substantially the same terms in both Resolutions and Treaty, they are the principles of free and common use, and of non-appropriation, of outer space and the celestial bodies.

But no definition of outer space, and no formal circumscription of its lower limits, are to be found in any of these instruments or as yet in accepted international usage. Nevertheless, two propositions can hardly be disputed: that a principle of free and common use precludes the *exclusive* jurisdiction of any State; and that a spacecraft in Earth orbit is already in outer space. The first proposition is really analytic, but the second needs some elaboration.

It might be argued that a spacecraft was not in outer space proper until it escaped from the gravitational control of the Earth, or that it was not on passage in outer space if it was designed for re-entry. But common sense would suggest that, just as airspace has come to be understood in terms of the functions of aircraft, so outer space is where spacecraft do their essential work, that is in orbit or beyond. That this view has won general acceptance, and is now part of international usage, can be demonstrated from the General Assembly Resolutions and the Outer Space Treaty. In the Resolutions we find Earth orbit and outer space plainly treated as equivalent.

So in Resolution 1721B–XVI the General Assembly

> *Believing* that the United Nations should provide a focal point for international co-operation in the . . . use of outer space,
>
> 1. *Calls upon* States launching objects into orbit . . .

to provide for their registration.

In Resolution 1802–XVII the General Assembly treated communication by Earth satellite as an important part of 'space communications'; and, even more plainly, in Resolution 1884–XVIII,

> 1. *Welcomes* the expressions by the U.S.S.R. and the U.S.A. of their intention not to station in outer space any objects carrying nuclear weapons . . .
> 2. *Solemnly calls upon all States*
> (*a*) to refrain from placing in orbit around the Earth any objects carrying nuclear weapons . . .

Again, under the Outer Space Treaty, satellites in Earth orbit must be regarded as in outer space, unless the unacceptable conclusion is to be drawn that assistance may be denied to astronauts, when they are in Earth orbit or have returned from orbit, and only granted when, under Article 5, they are or have been beyond, or that no liability for damage done by an object launched 'into outer space' is intended by Article 7 so long as it is placed only in orbit.

Further the reference in Article 4(1) to weapons placed in orbit around the Earth or stationed 'in outer space in any other manner' cannot be read, particularly in the light of Resolution 1884–XVIII, from which the provision is drawn, as intending a distinction between orbit and outer space.

However, the conclusion that satellites in Earth orbit are in outer space implies not that the lower limit of outer space is necessarily identical with the lowest effective orbiting altitude, but only that it is not higher.

With these preliminary remarks, we may then approach the problems of sovereignty and jurisdiction in space from two firm positions: that outer space is for common use and is incapable of appropriation so that no State may exercise *exclusive* jurisdiction over any part of it down at least to the lowest effective orbiting altitude; and that the celestial bodies, though physically capable of appropriation, have been declared *res communes* in absolute terms. What then are the limits of State jurisdiction?

The demarcation of territory on the surface of the earth does not present any great physical difficulties. Whether lines are to be drawn on land or on water, the combination of normally permanent physical features, as reference points, with accurate methods of surveying and measurement can yield clear and firm results. The space above the surface of the earth however presents two problems in any attempts at demarcation; a geometrical problem and a boundary problem.

The ancient *usque ad coelum* rule of Roman law rested on two presuppositions, of a fixed frame of spatial reference and of the impossibility of any human activity at more than a few hundred feet above the ground, and that only on a building. The Greek discovery of the sphericity of the Earth had been forgotten, and the movement of the Earth was not imagined. The concept of a fixed volume of space, occupied only by birds and a few tall buildings above a more or less flat and unmoving Earth, yielded therefore a rule of ownership of space that seemed as firmly based as that of the land itself.

The rotation and sphericity of the Earth makes the rule meaningless. Geometrically we may regard the Earth as motionless with space moving round it, or the Earth as rotating in a stationary volume of space; though there are reasons why one description is to be preferred to the other, both are accurate descriptions of the same physical facts. But whichever description is adopted it will be seen that no particular volume of space can be attached, in the sense of ownership, to any particular area of the surface of the Earth, since they are in constant relative movement. Space as such is therefore incapable of appropriation; and this is as true of the volume of space a few feet above the ground as it is of outer space. Further though the atmosphere rotates with the Earth the air-masses above its surface are in constant movement and do not respect any boundaries, so that no appropriation is possible of the air as such.

State sovereignty over the superjacent airspace, which is an established rule of international law, is therefore not *dominium* over it as a volume of air or of space, but rather *imperium* over activities or objectives above its territory, where 'above' is a defined geometrical relation between the activity or object and the territory; that is to say, the subjacent State alone can determine what activities may take place there and it has a right, in the absence of special agreement, to exclude any intruder, whether that intruder be a spacecraft, aircraft, radio wave, or noxious fumes.

Failure to make a similar distinction caused Lord Ellenborough to reject the impossibility of trespass to airspace. In ruling on the right of the defendant to affix to the wall of his house a wooden board overhanging the plaintiff's garden, he applied the test of *dominium* and plainly thought that airspace did not 'savour of the realty':

> Nay, if this board . . . be a trespass, it would follow that an aeronaut is liable to an action for trespass *quare clausum fregit* at the suit of the occupier of every field over which his balloon passes in the course of his voyage.[1]

Though the judgement is not good law,[2] it is a vivid expression of the power of the common law to simplify, and to bring under one legal concept the balloon, the aircraft, the spacecraft and the overhanging plank.

If then the description of the rights of a State above its territory is cast in terms of *imperium* over person, things and activities there, rather than *dominium* over a volume of space, it has some analogy with the 'sovereignty' of a coastal State over its continental shelf, as defined in the Continental Shelf Convention, Article 2.[3] Whether then exclusive jurisdiction and control above its territory is to be termed 'sovereignty' of the State is only a matter of terminology.

It remains to define what is meant by the expression 'above the territory' of a State. Geometrically again, and subject to any rule as to the upper limit of the airspace, an object is within this exclusive jurisdiction and control while its position is on any straight line drawn from the centre of the Earth and passing through a point in the surface territory of the subjacent State, including its territorial sea. The straight lines so drawn may be continued for great distances and the notion that the cone-like figures so established will overlap is fallacious; for the framework of reference is fixed, being defined by the centre of the Earth and an area of its surface, and the rotation of the Earth is here irrelevant. Within this frame of reference a spacecraft in synchronous orbit is stationary.

* * *

The boundary problem involves a number of distinct issues. Boundaries might be set in space for many different purposes: for example, spacecraft using nuclear fuels might be prohibited from operating below a certain altitude; launchers might be prohibited from dis-

[1] *Pickering v. Rudd* [1815] 4 *Camp.*, 217.

[2] *Kelsen v. Imperial Tobacco Co. Ltd* [1957] 2 *AER* 343.

[3] '1. The coastal State exercises over the continental shelf sovereign rights for the purpose of exploring it and exploiting its natural resources.'

charging waste in certain layers of the atmosphere; spacecraft returning to Earth might be required to travel in certain 'lanes'; an upper limit might be set to the right of states to control the use by spacecraft of their superjacent space; and whatever other limits were set, it might be agreed that no upper limit to the exercise of the right of self-defence by States would be recognized.

Let us take the issue of an upper limit to the exclusive jurisdiction and control of a State in the space above its territory, as the most general form of the boundary problem, and let us for the present limit the discussion to spacecraft, their operations and the effects of those operations; and I may remind you that spacecraft here include launchers and sounding rockets. Three questions arise: does a limit already exist in law; if not should any limit be set, and if so where?

But, in trying to answer these questions, we must keep firmly in mind that the limit we are seeking is that of the *exclusive* jurisdiction and control of States over objects and activity above their territories, and that this limit does not preclude other limits being set, or there being no limits, for other purposes.

In asking whether a limit already exists in law, we start from the position that a State has exclusive jurisdiction and control over objects in its superjacent airspace as we have defined it; it follows that spacecraft may not enter the airspace of a State without its authorization or consent. But there is no generally accepted legal definition of airspace, from which an upper limit to exclusive jurisdiction and control of the subjacent State can be deduced. From the accepted definition of 'aircraft', as a machine depending on the reactions of the air as its means of flight, some upper limits might be derived; so we might say that it was that altitude above the surface of the Earth at which an aircraft, depending both upon air breathing engines and aerodynamic lift, can no longer be operated. This may be of the order of twenty-five miles, though aerodynamic lift is not wholly lost until the region of the von Karman line is reached, at about fifty-two miles. Unless the notion of 'aircraft' then is to be strictly limited to conventional aircraft, the definition does not yield any firm upper limit, much less one that has been generally accepted.

From a certain absence of protest by States against the overflight of their territories by spacecraft it might be argued that a customary rule has already been established setting Earth satellites beyond their exclusive jurisdiction and control. But against this is the fact that certain kinds of satellite overflight have caused protests, and in any case States could hardly be taken to have acquiesced in overflights of which they have not had adequate notice, giving the elements and, in particular, the purpose of the flight.

However the adoption of the principles, that outer space is free for exploration and use by all States on a basis of equality[1] and in accordance with international law, and is not subject to national appropriation,[2] must be taken with some qualifications to have established a limit of exclusive jurisdiction and control. The resulting regime of outer space—we exclude for the moment the celestial bodies—is comparable to that of the high seas, of which the High Seas Convention, Article 2, says:

> The high seas being open to all nations, no State may validly purport to subject any part of them to its sovereignty. . . . These [four enumerated] freedoms and others which are recognized by the general principles of international law shall be exercised by all States with reasonable regard to the interests of other States in their exercise of the freedom of the high seas.

The only way in which any part of outer space could be appropriated by a State would be by its effectively denying access to it of spacecraft of other States; and free exploration and use entail that every part of outer space shall be open under international law to all spacecraft without interference. It follows that the principles of free use and non-appropriation must come in practice to have much the same consequences and implications as the freedom of the high seas: no State can exercise exclusive jurisdiction or control, so as to deny or interfere with the access of any spacecraft to any part of outer space. But two qualifications are necessary: first, under Resolution 1962–XVIII and the Treaty, the State of registry retains jurisdiction and control over a spacecraft when in outer space, which is analogous to that of the flag State over a ship on its registry; and secondly, a State may exercise such rights of self-defence in outer space as are recognized by international law, including the United Nations Charter. We may say then that, subject to these two qualifications, the lower limit of outer space in relation to the Earth

[1] Resolution 1962–XVIII, paragraph 2, repeated in Outer Space Treaty, Article 1(2), with the addition of the words 'without discrimination of any kind'.
[2] Ibid., paragraph 3, repeated verbatim in Outer Space Treaty, Article 2.

must, in absence of any other agreed limit, constitute the upper limit of the exclusive jurisdiction and control of States over objects above their territory.

But the lower limit or boundary of outer space remains in law undetermined. Is it necessary for such a limit to be set, and if so where is it to be? Exclusive jurisdiction and control by a State over activities and objects in its superjacent space may be said to have four main purposes: defence, the prevention of nuisance, the maintenance of good order, and the avoidance of economic competition. Nuisance would include disturbance of the atmosphere and nuclear radiation; good order would include the avoidance of navigational hazards in the airspace or above, and interference with radio communications; economic competition also could arise in the commercial uses of spacecraft.

Many suggestions have been made for the determination of the upper limit of exclusive jurisdiction and control over objects in space based on the aviation conventions, the physical character of airspace, the function and performance of 'flight instrumentalities', the limits of effective control, or arbitrarily chosen altitudes.[1] Indeed there is now ample basis for a choice, though to be effective it can only be made by international agreement. What I hope to have established is simply that, though the *upper limit of exclusive* jurisdiction and control may be set lower, it cannot now be regarded as higher, than the effective orbiting altitude of Earth satellites.

But even this limit is imprecise, and could be determined in at least three possible ways. A spacecraft could be deemed to enter outer space at the point at which it passed into orbit around the Earth; the boundary of outer space would then be determined afresh for each spacecraft, whether it remained in orbit or passed from it further into outer space. This inconvenience could be avoided by generalizing orbiting altitude and declaring the boundary of outer space to be a sphere, with its centre at the centre of the Earth, and at a distance from the surface equal to the lowest perigee[2] altitude of spacecraft in effective orbit around the Earth. This method would

[1] As summarized in McDougal, Lasswell and Vlasic, ***Law and Public Order in Space*** (Yale University Press, 1963), 323f.

[2] Perigee is the point in the orbit around the Earth, of the Moon or an artificial satellite, at which the body makes its closest approach to the Earth; apogee is the point in the orbit of greatest distance.

not in itself yield a precise boundary altitude for outer space, though it would be of the order of one hundred miles. Few Earth satellites have had a perigee altitude below that, and for the greatest number it is higher, since below it atmospheric drag progressively diminishes the effective life of a satellite in orbit. A third method, by which the boundary of outer space could be fixed arbitrarily at one hundred miles and which is essentially a precise form of the second, is perhaps then to be preferred.

The first method of determination differs from the others in that it is capable of evolving, and may already be evolving, as a customary rule; the other methods depend essentially on international agreement.

But if this boundary came by one method or another to be accepted, there could be problems of the access of spacecraft to outer space and of their return to Earth, if overflight were necessary of the territory of a State other than the operating State, and *below* the boundary of outer space. These problems have not, it appears, yet arisen in practice owing to the geographical position of launching sites at present in use. But neither the General Assembly Resolutions nor the Outer Space Treaty deal with them directly. A right of innocent airflight would have to be established by special agreement or by a general convention. Here the notion of 'innocent' would no doubt comprise at least registration of the characteristics of the spacecraft, its flight elements, and purpose of its flight, with the U.N. as under the present system; observance of any conditions necessary to safety of navigation in the airspace; and absence of any prejudice to the good order or security of the subjacent State.

* * *

Turning now to the freedoms of outer space itself and its common use, we find that, like most freedoms, they are not absolute. The Resolutions and the Treaty and customary law combine to establish certain liabilities, prohibitions and obligations, which may come to rank with the two principles already discussed, as rules of law. First, the ascent of a spacecraft to outer space and its return to Earth are subject to the conditions[1] that the operator is responsible for its movement and control, and is liable for damage that may result, and that it may not enter the airspace of a State without its authorization

[1] Resolution 1962–XVIII, para. 8; Outer Space Treaty, Art. 7.

or consent. The responsible operator must be understood to include the State launching, or procuring the launch of a spacecraft, and also the State from whose territory it is launched, if different. Further, the State remains internationally responsible whether the operation is conducted by it or by a private agency.

Second, the free and common use of outer space and the celestial bodies is limited by prohibitions against appropriation or claims of appropriation; against the stationing of weapons in orbit or on celestial bodies;[1] and against certain military uses of celestial bodies.[2] Third, the responsible operator must exercise due diligence to avoid contamination of outer space or the celestial bodies;[3] or the introduction into the environment of the Earth of extraterrestrial matter, which may cause adverse changes;[4] or potentially harmful interference with the lawful uses of outer space by other operators,[5] which must be taken to include interference with access to and navigation in outer space, as well as interference with legitimate scientific experiments or observations.

The celestial bodies differ from space in that they are capable, at least in theory, of physical appropriation by modes similar to the acquisition of title to territory on the Earth. But claims of national appropriation are eliminated by Resolution 1962–XVIII and the Outer Space Treaty, and the principles of free exploration, use, and access to all areas substituted.

Free use and access appear to mean in the case of a celestial body freedom for a spacecraft to fly by or go into orbit around it, or to make a landing upon it, and freedom to make use of it and its resources, subject to certain restrictions in the Resolutions and the Treaty.

The celestial bodies, to which space operations are likely to be directed for some time to come, are in order of their closest approach to the Earth, the Moon, certain planetoids, Venus and Mars. They vary much in their hospitality and scope for exploration. Venus, with its dense atmosphere and high surface temperature, discourages manned landings. Planetoids, such as Eros, Hermes and Icarus and others, which come from time to time within the orbit of the Earth,

[1] Resolution 1844–XVIII, para. 2(*a*); Outer Space Treaty, Art. 4(1).
[2] Treaty, Art. 4(2).
[3] Ibid., Art. 9(2).
[4] Ibid., Art. 4(2).
[5] Resolution 1962–XVIII, para. 6; Treaty, Art. 9(3) and (4).

may serve as platforms for observational instruments, or for take-off by spacecraft on more distant journeys. The Moon and Mars offer more immediate prospects of exploration; though it has not yet been demonstrated what the one, described by Professor Hoyle as a slag-heap, or the other, a crater-strewn desert with perhaps some lowly vegetation, have to offer, commensurate with the fantastic cost of getting there.

The outer planets present formidable difficulties of navigational approach, let alone landings of space probes, unmanned or manned. The journey to Jupiter of a space probe, moving on a path tangential to the orbits of the Earth and Jupiter, would take about two and three-quarter years; and a fast hyperbolic path, still far beyond the present capacity of chemical propulsion of rockets, would take not less than a year to traverse. Further, the space probe would have the hazard of crossing the belt of thousands of planetoids between Mars and Jupiter; though, as their mean plane is at a higher inclination to the ecliptic than Jupiter, it might with extra fuel be able to duck under.

If men are to attempt the journey to Mars or beyond, more may need to be learnt about the effects of weightlessness, and of confinement in a small space, over such long periods. The voyage to Mars will be exacting enough, even if the seven months' journey-time of Mariner IV were to be halved.

The legal implications of human travel beyond the solar system are not made a matter of sensible discourse merely by calling them metalaw. Even if the attainment of relativistic speeds were to make this travel possible, it is idle now to try to legislate for the strange encounters that might result; suppose the nearest star and its hypothetical planets are composed of anti-matter.[1]

Let us return to the more homely region of the inner planets and planetoids. Freedom of access to all parts of these bodies, which is established by Article (1)2 of the Treaty, must include freedom of approach from orbit and movement over the surface. But it is qualified by the principles of Article 8 that jurisdiction and control over a spacecraft and its personnel, is retained by the State of registry

[1] This theoretical possibility is discussed in Hannes Alfven, Professor of Plasma Physics in the Royal Institute of Technology, Stockholm, *Worlds—Antiworlds* (W. H. Freeman & Co., 1966).

even when the spacecraft is on a celestial body, and by the principle of mutual non-interference in Article 9(2).

If we may speculate a little on the position of a station on the Moon or Mars, it would, whether manned or unmanned, need freedom from interference with communications between it and the Earth and with any observations, physical or astronomical it was making; if manned there would be need for free movement around it and for use of any mineral resources in its vicinity, that might serve as fuel. It is difficult then to see how a permanent station could be maintained without some form of tenure of the ground on or under which it was placed, and of an area around it sufficient for its maintenance and effective use, and also of necessary rights of way. The essential elements of such tenure would perhaps be that the station should be permanent, in the sense that, whether affixed to the ground or not, it was not to be brought back to Earth; that its establishment and the area required for its maintenance and use should be notified to the Secretary-General of the United Nations; that the area so notified should be reasonably proportionate to the size, functions and needs of the station; that the station and the area notified would be under the exclusive jurisdiction of the State of registry of the spacecraft bringing the component parts of the station;[1] and tenure would be for the duration of the active use of the station. Rights of jurisdiction and control of the station could be assigned to another state or an international organization by agreement, registrable under Article 102 of the Charter.

If I may now summarize this intricate discussion:

1. The rights of a State in the space above its territory are best expressed in terms of exclusive jurisdiction and control, rather than of sovereignty, if sovereignty is understood as involving *dominium* as well as *imperium*;

2. Jurisdiction and control is exclusive in the sense that the subjacent State may deny access to or use of the space above its territory, or may subject it to conditions;

3. The upper limit of exclusive jurisdiction and control is now determined by the general recognition that spacecraft in Earth orbit or beyond are in outer space;

4. This upper limit does not affect the rights of the subjacent State to

[1] Article 8 of the Treaty appears to mean this. 'A State party to the Treaty on whose registry an object launched into outer space is carried shall retain jurisdiction and control over such an object . . . on a celestial body.' Ownership of 'objects landed, or constructed on a celestial body, including their component parts' is also retained.

exercise jurisdiction and control over spacecraft on its registry, or to take measures of legitimate self-defence, in outer space;

5. The upper limit is still capable of more precise definition;

6. The exercise of exclusive jurisdiction and control over objects and activities in space *below* the upper limit remains subject to all applicable rules of international law.

Chapter III

FORCE

It is plain that the inspiration for space activities has been so far predominantly military. For the needs of what is commonly described as defence, there is among the space-users a deployment of men, money and resources on a vast scale, which scientific or technological research in any field could not alone have hoped to command. But there is a contradiction in the uses of outer space: for as the potential dangers of the military uses increase, so does the need and demand for limiting or avoiding them. In every space administration there are armers and disarmers side by side; with its right hand it devises extensions of military capabilities and, with its left hand, means of defence against them. So when President Johnson describes the Outer Space Treaty as 'the most important arms-control development since the limited test-ban treaty of 1963', it behoves us also to see what room for manœuvre in outer space the Treaty has left for the military. I shall consider then, among the uses of outer space, the use or threat of force, demilitarization and self-defence.

Space operations may be a manifest use or threat of force, contrary to Article 2(4) of the Charter, or they may have a scientific or commercial purpose and yet be capable of easy conversion to military use. The preambles of both Resolution 1962–XVIII and the Treaty stress the interest of mankind in the exploration and use for peaceful purposes, and Article 4 of the Treaty, which we shall discuss later, provides that the celestial bodies shall be 'used exclusively for peaceful purposes'. The difficulties presented by the expression 'peaceful purposes' are well-known.[1] 'Peaceful' may in describing space operations mean simply 'non-aggressive' and could then include any manner of defence; or, much more restrictedly, 'non-military'. 'Purposes' may relate to the immediate use only or be extended to cover any capability of a particular device or operation. Further, since

[1] See in the war space context R. Gardner, 'Cooperation in Outer Space', 41 *Foreign Affairs* [1963] 349.

almost any technical device is capable, directly or by adaptation, of being put to some military use, it is difficult and often impossible to characterize its invention, construction or use, as being exclusively non-military or military. Among the military uses of spacecraft and stations, we find their use as missiles or other weapons; as anti-missile missiles or as inspection satellites; as missile bases; as reconnaissance satellites; or as a communications point in a weapon or command system.

While anti-missile missiles in orbit and inspection satellites may be regarded solely as means of defence and so non-aggressive, though military, there are also devices, which though not weapons of mass destruction are not solely defensive: for example, a recent development is MIRV (Multiple Individually-targetable Re-entry Vehicle), a spacecraft designed to carry both ballistic missiles, which may be aimed in any direction, and decoys launched to confuse radar and other tracking systems. Ambiguous also are reconnaissance satellites and spacecraft or stations used as communications points, and the use of reconnaissance satellites has been, prior to the Outer Space Treaty, controversial.[1]

A United States Deputy Secretary of Defense stated before a Congressional Committee that no objection could be raised in law, if the Soviet Union placed a reconnaissance satellite in orbit so as to traverse the United States.[2] In support of this position it has been said that the manner of observation is itself peaceful, and that it may be compared with the observation of territory by eye, binoculars or camera, from the sea or on the land itself. This, like other forms of espionage in time of peace, is said to be not contrary to international law, even though it may in some cases be a breach of the domestic law of the territory.

But even if the information obtained by a man sitting on the waterfront at Algeciras, watching shipping movements in Gibraltar harbour through binoculars, can be seriously compared with that obtained by a superlative high-definition camera, sweeping daily over millions of square miles of territory, the argument is not convincing. It may in general be asked why the deliberate breach by one State

[1] See generally J. F. McMahon, 'Legal Controls of Outer Space', 38 *BYIL* [1962] 339.

[2] Jessup and Taubenfeld, *Controls for Outer Space* (1960), 217; cited McMahon, op. cit.

of the domestic law of another State is not contrary to international law. Further, the Chicago Convention 1944 contains provisions which read together might be said to cover *in principle* the use of reconnaissance satellites:

> Article 8. No aircraft capable of being flown without a pilot shall be flown without a pilot over the territory of a contracting State without special authorization by that State . . .
>
> Article 36. Each contracting State may prohibit or regulate the use of photographic apparatus in aircraft over its territory.

But is a satellite an aircraft capable of being flown without a pilot? There is no definition of an aircraft in the Chicago Convention, and since it is concerned largely with civil aviation, it might be said that 'aircraft' in the Convention means 'conventional aircraft'. But no civil aircraft existed in 1944, or is likely to exist for some time, operated without a pilot, and therefore in Article 8 the term 'aircraft' might be capable of a wider meaning covering the form of pilotless aircraft in use as a 'flying bomb', which certainly depended for its flight upon the reactions of the air. Article 36 does not exclude from its scope aircraft flown without a pilot, and in neither Article is the expression 'over the territory' limited in altitude. But against any such reasoning stands the fact that State practice since 1957 shows no move to extend the concept of aircraft to include spacecraft proper, at least in the contexts of the Chicago Convention; though it is strange that a rule should be accepted forbidding unauthorized photography from aircraft, including pilotless aircraft, but that there should be no rule prohibiting the far more efficient photographic reconnaissance by satellite. The U-2 aircraft can hardly be distinguished from the reconnaissance satellite solely on the ground that its photography was an incident of intrusion into foreign airspace, while that of the satellite is an incident of the free use of outer space. We shall return to the use of reconnaissance satellites in the context of the Outer Space Treaty.

A satellite or a station on Earth or on a celestial body may be part of a communications system, which is integrated, or is capable of quick integration, with a weapon or military command system. The difficulty of determining whether it is military or non-military, and if military whether it is defensive or aggressive, is illustrated by the protest by the Soviet Union to Norway in 1965 against the establishment by ESRO (European Space Research Organization) of a satellite tracking station in Spitsbergen.[1] The Soviet Union argued that, since it was capable of military use and in particular of reconnaissance by satellite of the Soviet Union, it was contrary to the demilitarization provisions of the Spitsbergen Treaty 1920. Norway rejected the protest on the ground that ESRO was using the station for the exclusively peaceful purposes of scientific research.

*   *   *

Let us now look at the Outer Space Treaty. It provides for a partial demilitarization of outer space and the celestial bodies, and for this purpose treats them differently.

The demilitarization of outer space does not go beyond the exclusion of certain kinds of weapon. Article 4(1) provides that:

> States parties to the treaty undertake not to place in orbit around the Earth any objects carrying nuclear weapons or any other kinds of weapons of mass destruction, . . . or station such weapons in outer space in any other manner.

This is in substance identical with General Assembly Resolution 1884–XVIII, paragraph 2(*a*), and is declaratory of international law, as already described. What *Izvestia* claimed to be orbital weapons appeared in the Moscow Anniversary parade in November 1965, but it is possible that the principal space-users were able to reach agreement on the disuse of spacecraft as carriers at least of weapons of mass destruction. This may in part have been because their manipulation and control was likely to be at best hazardous, their capability was not greater than the ICBM, and technical developments had shown them to be vulnerable to interference by States threatened.

But Article 4 of the Treaty does not prohibit the use of spacecraft in orbit around the Earth, or even perhaps a celestial body, having reconnaissance, anti-missile, communications, or other military, functions. The manned satellite in particular, because of the advantage of flexibility of choice and decision, which a man still has over a machine, is likely to be an essential part of future weapons systems.

The absence from the Treaty of any prohibition of reconnaissance satellites, or even of direct reference to them, is striking. One of two

[1] Described by I. Brownlie, 'The Maintenance of Peace in Outer Space', 40 *BYIL* [1964] 5.

inferences may be drawn: that the principal space-users have come to acquiesce in the use of reconnaissance satellites,[1] or that the issue remains open and that reliance might be put on the provision of Article 3 of the Treaty, that space activities shall be carried on 'in accordance with international law', to argue that reconnaissance by satellite is unlawful.

The Soviet Union, despite a good deal of grumbling and charges of aggression by its legal writers and representatives in United Nations debates, did not go so far, in its Draft Declaration on the uses of outer space,[2] as to say that the use of reconnaissance satellites was contrary to international law. There it declared that:

> 8. The use of artificial satellites for the collection of intelligence information in the territory of foreign states is incompatible with the objectives of mankind in its conquest of outer space.

Such satellites, the declaration added, should not if captured be returned to the State of origin. It may be that this guarded declaration reflected the development by the Soviet Union of efficient reconnaissance satellites.

There is reason then to think that reconnaissance satellites are now established as legitimate, whatever earlier arguments may have been raised against them; and they are even perhaps in the interest of mankind in that they represent an efficient form of inspection of military activities, and the avoidance of inspection has always been a major obstacle to disarmament.

* * *

For the Moon and other celestial bodies, the Treaty has established a more complete form of demilitarization. Article 4(2) reads:

> The Moon and other celestial bodies shall be used by all States parties to the Treaty exclusively for peaceful purposes. The establishment of military bases, installations, and fortifications, the testing of any type of weapons, and the conduct of military manœuvres on celestial bodies shall be forbidden. The use of military personnel for scientific research or for any other peaceful purposes shall not be prohibited. The use of any equipment or facility necessary for peaceful exploration of the Moon and other celestial bodies shall also not be prohibited.

[1] There is good reason to believe that the territories of the Soviet Union and the United States, and no doubt others, are under more or less continuous observation by American and Russian satellites respectively.

[2] U.N. Doc. A/AC.105/L.2 (10.9.1962): quoted by McMahon, op. cit.

Here we are faced with the question whether purposes are only peaceful, if they are non-military, or are sufficiently peaceful if they are non-aggressive. The paragraph is plainly modelled on Article I of the Antarctica Treaty 1959,[1] but is not so widely phrased. In Antarctica all measures of a military nature are prohibited, examples being given. In Article 4(2) of the Outer Space Treaty we have only the examples, to which military installations are added. It is not clear then whether the establishment of military bases, the testing of weapons and so on, are explanatory examples of non-peaceful purposes, so that 'peaceful' would mean in effect 'non-military'; or whether those activities alone are prohibited, and other activities having a military purpose, for example, defence, are not excluded. If the first interpretation was intended, why was the language of Antarctica Convention, Article 9, changed when taken into the Outer Space Treaty? Again, if the second interpretation is followed, is it permissible for defence purposes to place military satellites in orbit round the Moon or another celestial body?

Finally, while in Antarctica the use of military personnel or equipment is permitted for any peaceful purpose, a distinction, which tends to support the second interpretation, is made between them in their use on the Moon or other celestial bodies. The use of military personnel for any peaceful purpose is permitted, as in the Antarctica Convention, and is natural, given the present form of management of space operations; but in the provision that

> The use of any equipment or facility necessary for peaceful exploration of the Moon or other celestial bodies shall also not be prohibited . . .

the expression 'any equipment' must include military equipment, but the use of equipment is separated from peaceful purposes, and if necessary to peaceful exploration, other uses are not excluded, such as defence.

The Article as a whole gives the impression that a more limited demilitarization of the Moon and other celestial bodies was intended than of Antarctica, and that their use for peaceful purposes does not

[1] '1. Antarctica shall be used for peaceful purposes only. There shall be prohibited *inter alia* any measures of a military nature, such as the establishment of military bases and fortifications, the carrying out of military manœuvres, as well as the testing of any type of weapons.

2. The present Treaty shall not prevent the use of military personnel or equipment for scientific research or for any other peaceful purpose.'

exclude measures of defence, for example, the incorporation of stations on them in missile warning or satellite inspection systems.

It is perhaps a mistake to press these points of interpretation too far, but in an instrument of the supposed importance of the Outer Space Treaty, some care and precision of language may be expected. An oddity here is the omission of the Moon from the critical provision in Article 4(2) prohibiting the establishment of military bases and so on. This provision as it stands covers only celestial bodies. Does this expression include the Moon in this context? Instead of a definitions clause, that might have been expected, the stock phrase 'outer space, including the Moon and other celestial bodies' is used twenty-two times in thirteen Articles, and its components are sometimes used separately. So in Article 4(2) itself the expression 'the Moon and other celestial bodies' appears twice save in the central sentence, where the omission of the Moon must either be intentional, or an egregious mistake, only to be saved by saying that the whole tenor requires that the expression 'celestial bodies' in that sentence must include the Moon.

* * *

The control of demilitarization of the celestial bodies and of the placing of weapons of mass destruction in orbit is supplied in part by provisions for observation and inspection. Article 10 reads:

> In order to promote international co-operation in the peaceful exploration and use of outer space, including the Moon and other celestial bodies, in conformity with the purposes of this Treaty, the States parties to the Treaty shall consider on a basis of equality any requests by other States parties to the Treaty to be afforded an opportunity to observe the flight of space objects launched by those States. The nature of such an opportunity for observation and the conditions under which it could be afforded shall be determined by agreement between the States concerned.

This Article lays down three conditions: first, that requests for observation shall be received and considered without discrimination between States. Second, as a *pactum de contrahendo*, that the opportunity and conditions of observation shall be determined by agreement. It is to be presumed that such an agreement will be negotiated in good faith and with due regard to the purposes of the Treaty, but the Treaty is silent about the consequences of refusal to agree. Third, the opportunity must be given 'to observe the flight of space objects'.

Article 10 is essentially a provision for the establishment of spacecraft tracking facilities, and States undertake to co-operate in the stationing of tracking units in their various territories. There is an element of inspection here for in Article 11, with the same introductory words as Article 10, the States parties to the treaty agree to make the task of tracking easier by informing

> the Secretary-General of the United Nations as well as the public and the international scientific community to the greatest extent feasible and practicable, of the nature, conduct, locations, and results, of such activities.

This reiterates in broad terms the principle of General Assembly Resolution 1721B–XVI, calling upon

> States launching objects into orbit or beyond to furnish information promptly to the Committee on the Peaceful Uses of Outer Space through the Secretary-General, for the registration of launchings . . .[1]

and the practice noted by the General Assembly in Resolution 1884–XVIII by which

> certain Member States have, on a voluntary basis, provided information on their national space programmes.

It is however well known that by no means all spacecraft launchings have been registered with the Secretary-General.

Means of inspection on the celestial bodies are provided in Article 2:

> All stations, installations, equipment and space vehicles on the Moon and other celestial bodies shall be open to representatives of other States parties to the Treaty, on a basis of reciprocity. Such representatives shall give reasonable advance notice of a projected visit . . .

The condition of reciprocity is an odd limitation. If the principle of open inspection is accepted, it seems unnecessary, since each contracting State would be bound by the rule. If however a State is bound to permit inspection, only on the basis of reciprocity, it may refuse inspection on the ground that equivalent conditions of inspection are not offered in return. In practice the condition would, if strictly applied, limit inspection to the principal space-users; that is to say, for the present and for some time to come the only States able to claim rights inspection under Article 12 would be the United

[1] The existence of the registry was noted by the General Assembly in December 1963: Resolution 1884–XVIII (II).

States and the Soviet Union. Reciprocity may however be meant to imply no more than that arrangements for inspection shall be matters for bilateral agreement; and here we may recall the large number of agreements concluded by the United States for the delivery of nuclear materials, equipment and devices to other countries, and inspections carried out under these agreements.

The system of inspection contemplated by Article 12 of the Treaty appears to be one of individual observers, modelled on that suitable on or near the ground in Antarctica; and it may be asked whether effective inspection will not be better carried out by tracking stations or by satellites themselves, equipped to detect and interpret the electronic processes in the spacecraft to be observed, and whether for this inspection the procedure of request or advance notice will be necessary or even enforceable. Indeed it seems that the necessary interference with the movement of shipping on the high seas which the right of visit and search must involve, so that its exercise is strictly limited, has no analogy here: for space inspection can be carried out without any interference with movement at all.

It may also be asked whether inspection of all spacecraft, whether in outer space or on celestial bodies is not best placed in the hands of an international agency. Article 12 like the rest of the Treaty studiously ignores the United Nations and the belief of the General Assembly that

> the United Nations should provide a focal point for international co-operation in the peaceful exploration and use of outer space.[1]

Even if the United Nations were to embark itself on space operations it would have under the Treaty no right of inspection.

* * *

It remains to ask what counteraction is possible against military uses of outer space or the celestial bodies which are contrary to the Treaty or otherwise unlawful? Here the right of self-defence, recognized in Article 51 of the Charter, has primacy, since its field is not necessarily limited like that of security jurisdiction or territorial jurisdiction.

The meaning of the first sentence of Article 51, and in particular

[1] Resolution 1721B–XVI.

of the words 'in case of armed attack', is not free from doubt. Two approaches appear possible and we will take them in turn. The first is to regard the sentence as in part a statement about the place in international law of self-defence. The words 'in the case of armed attack' are not then simply setting out one of the conditions, doubtless the most characteristic, in which the right of self-defence is exercised, but are describing the extent of the right itself, and are in fact limiting its exercise to situations of armed attack. In short, the sentence is to be read as declaratory of the extent of the right of self-defence in international law, and it has been argued that by 1945 its limitation to situations of armed attack had become a customary rule.[1] If it is declaratory, the first sentence is highly telescoped, and has to be read as saying 'The right of individual or collective self-defence is limited to cases of armed attack, and this right shall not be impaired by any provision of the Charter'. It is difficult to believe that so important a declaration would be so made. Further, if it is declaratory, the qualification of armed attack as being on a Member of the United Nations would be unnecessary.

But there is another approach, which I suggest avoids these difficulties and is to be preferred. The first sentence of Article 51, if read as a whole, may be seen to be, not a statement about the character or extent of the right of self-defence at all, but a statement of the relationship between the Security Council and Members of the United Nations, acting individually or collectively, in dealing with breaches of the peace or aggression. So the primary responsibility of the Security Council in these cases, which is indeed firmly asserted in Article 51, is not to deprive Members of their right to defend themselves and each other[2] until the Security Council takes effective charge of the situation. Our conclusion would then be that Article 51 covers the respective rights and duties under Chapter VII of the Security Council on the one hand and Members of the United Nations on the other, where an armed attack, constituting a breach of the peace or aggression, occurs; but that the extent of the inherent right

[1] I. Brownlie, *International Law and the Use of Force by States* (Oxford University Press, 1963), Ch. XIII.

[2] The qualification of attack as being on a Member of the United Nations perhaps reflects the fact that Article 51, was originally designed to cover peace-keeping arrangements for and between countries of a region; the concept of regional participation was then, on transfer of the Article into Chapter VII, translated into United Nations Membership.

of self-defence is left open by the Article, and in particular whether it includes a right to use force in anticipation of an armed attack, or in situations other than armed attack.

An armed attack, a breach of the peace or act of aggression, are processes in time, and not instantaneous events characterized, as it were, by the first explosion; they may even achieve their purpose without a shot being fired. The length of the process must vary with the area of the attack and the instruments employed, and will be slower on land or sea than in the air or outer space. Self-defence must, if it is to serve its purpose, be a simultaneous process in time; a mobilization of forces, a state of readiness, a strike at the opposing forces. But the use of force in self-defence must be controlled by the principle of proportionality. It must correspond with the attack in the kind of force employed; it must be proportionate to the attack in the degree of force used; and it must be reasonably co-extensive in time and place with the attack. Where a strike is made at the opposing force, in face of a clear and present danger of attack, which has become manifest through the interception of communications, observation of the character or movement of the opposing force, or other intelligence, it is still limited by Article 2(4) of the Charter, and in particular the purposes of the United Nations, and by the requirements of Article 51. The military capabilities of spacecraft have not only enlarged by many magnitudes the possible range and scale of attack, but have reduced the time process of its preparation and delivery from months or weeks to minutes.[1] The scope of self-defence must be extended proportionately though not, paradoxically perhaps, in the scale of response.

Its extension would necessarily preclude the setting of any upper limit above the surface of the Earth on the legitimate exercise of the right of self-defence, nor is there any provision of the Charter or rule of customary law imposing such a limit. Further, the placing of a nuclear weapon or other weapon of mass destruction in orbit in breach of the Outer Space Treaty might with reason be regarded as an initiation of armed attack, and given the potentialities of such a weapon as a general threat justifying collective defence. 'Weapons of mass destruction' are not defined in the Outer Space Treaty or

[1] E.g. the development in orbital weapons overcoming their technical and tactical deficiencies.

in Resolution 1884–XVIII, but the Institute of International Law has described such a weapon as follows:

Doit être considéré comme destruction massive, l'anéantissement de tout groupe d'hommes sans distinction possible entre membres des forces militaires et population civile, ainsi que l'anéantissement de tout centre urbain ou rural ou de toute région sans distinction possible entre objectifs militaires et non militaires . . .

Further

Est interdit par le droit international public en vigueur l'emploi de toute arme dont l'action nocive pourrait, de par sa nature et déjá sans les conditions normales, échapper, dans l'espace ou dans le temps, au contrôle de ceux qui l'emploient et ne permet plus, pour cette raison, une distinction entre membres des forces militaires et population civile ou entre objectifs militaires et non militaires.

Any State then would, on the foregoing reasoning, be entitled to take counter-action against such a weapon placed in orbit on two conditions: that it was limited to removing the immediate danger, by diversion, neutralization or if necessary, destruction of the satellite itself; and that an immediate report was made to the Security Council under Article 51. Article 2(4) would, it is believed, preclude a strike against any terrestrial control point. At least two weapons systems, able to intercept and destroy satellites, have already been established, under the operational control of the United States Continental Air Defense Command.

What counter-action may be taken against space operations, which are regarded as hostile, though they are not precipitating an armed attack, or which are contrary to the principles of Resolution 1962–XVIII or the provisions of the Treaty?

The alleged hostile character of a spacecraft is properly a matter of the Security Council and for a determination as to whether its operation is a threat to the peace under Article 39. If the Council so determined, it could decide upon diversion of the spacecraft under Article 41, or its capture or destruction under Article 42.

But given the uncertainty of such a decision being taken in the presence of the principal space-users, and the fact that not all breaches of the Treaty would be threats to the peace, enforcement of the Treaty may have to depend in large part on customary international law, or new principles yet to be evolved, consistent with the U.N. Charter. Two situations at least have to be covered: the use of

Earth satellites, and the establishment of stations on celestial bodies or of satellites around them. Security zones based on some form of State jurisdiction would, it seems, be impracticable for coping with Earth satellites. Even if the vague notion of 'security'[1] is replaced by that of a breach or suspected breach of the Treaty, the velocity of spacecraft, for which there is no terrestrial analogy at all, would make zonal control impossible for any but the territorially largest States.

The control of Earth satellites is a global problem and any attempt to solve it regionally, let alone in terms of State jurisdiction, is likely to create more conflicts than it avoids. The following considerations are perhaps material. First, any breach or suspected breach of the Treaty by the use of an Earth satellite is a matter in which all States parties have a common interest,[2] so that any State may take action upon it whether directly affected or not. Second, a distinction should be made between spacecraft not designed for controlled re-entry, unmanned spacecraft designed for controlled re-entry, and manned spacecraft so designed. In the first case, the only course possible is direct interference with the spacecraft by diversion, capture or destruction. In the other cases, however, the launching State could be required to bring the spacecraft down, so that direct interference would not be justifiable unless the requirement had not been met; this would apply even more strongly, in common humanity, to manned spacecraft.

Spacecraft emitting hostile propaganda in time of peace are condemned by General Assembly Resolution 110–II[3] and, more obliquely, by the Outer Space Treaty, which cites that Resolution in its preamble but otherwise leaves the problem to be covered by the general provisions of Articles 1 and 3.

[1] For its inadequacy and rejection in the case of the sea, see I. Brownlie, *International Law and the Use of Force by States*, op. cit., at 4–5. Air identification zones, as established by the United States and Canada, provide no real analogy.

[2] See in particular Article 9(1): 'In the exploration and use of outer space, including the Moon and other celestial bodies, States parties to the Treaty shall be guided by the principle of cooperation and a mutual assistance and shall conduct all their activities in outer space, including the Moon and other celestial bodies, with due regard to the corresponding interests of all other States parties to the treaty;' and generally Articles 1 and 3.

[3] Contrast the abortive Hague Air Warfare Rules (1923), Art. 21: 'The use of aircraft for the purpose of disseminating propaganda shall not be treated as an illegitimate means of warfare.'

The establishment of stations on the Moon or other celestial bodies contrary to the Treaty, and in particular Article 4, poses the question whether, failing effective action by the Security Council under either Chapter VI or Chapter VII, the use of force against them is precluded by Article 2(4) of the Charter. I believe that the answer must be that it is not, since the purposes of the Charter would have been served, as far as was possible, by reference of the situation to the Security Council; and action against such stations could not infringe the territorial integrity of a State, given the principle of non-appropriation. Any right of tenure in the station, regarded as territorial by analogy, would be terminated by its unlawful use.

Chapter IV

ORGANIZATION

To turn now from force to order, we must see what part law can play in the organization and control of the uses of outer space. Space operations depend far more upon technology than upon pure science, and they form an organic part of the industrial and social framework from which they have sprung. They must be governed then at many points by the same rules of law as govern the operations of any large industrial enterprise, public or private. Since they can be carried on only on a global scale, and their fruits good or bad are distributed over the Earth, they are essentially international. We have an area therefore where law, international and municipal, industrial organization, and social policy are closely engaged together, and where some of the traditional distinction between international law and municipal law will be broken down.

The U.N. Committee on the Peaceful Uses of Outer Space recommended[1] that a world conference might be held late in 1967 to consider developments in the uses of outer space, and the fields which it chose show the range and influence of space activities. They were communications, including the use of mass communications for education and as aids to technical development; meteorology; air and sea navigation; geodetic surveys; biology, and in particular the applications of space medicine; education and training for space operations; and finally, what used to be known as 'fall-out' and is now called 'spin-off', the technological and scientific by-products of the whole space enterprise, in the form of new techniques and adaptations.

As selection is inevitable, I propose to discuss in the remaining lectures some of the legal aspects of the organization of space activities, and particularly space communications; and some of the side-effects of space operations.

Both Resolution 1962–XVIII and Article 6 of the Outer Space

[1] Report of the Working Group of the Whole: U.N. Doc. A/AC.105/34.

Treaty establish the principle of State responsibility for space operations. Article 6, resuming the language of paragraph 5 of the Resolution, provides:

States parties to the treaty shall bear international responsibility for national activities in outer space, including the Moon and other celestial bodies, whether such activities are carried on by governmental agencies or by non-governmental entities, and for assuring that national activities are carried out in conformity with the provisions set forth in the present treaty.

The activities of non-governmental entities in outer space, including the Moon and other celestial bodies, shall require authorization and continuing supervision by the State concerned. When activities are carried on in outer space, including the Moon and other celestial bodies, by an international organization, responsibility for compliance with this treaty shall be borne both by the international organization and by the States parties to the treaty participating in such organization.

Article 7 reads:

Each State party to the treaty that launches or procures the launching of an object into outer space, including the Moon and other celestial bodies, and each State party from whose territory or facility an object is launched, is internationally liable for damage to another State party to the treaty or to its natural or juridical persons by such object or its component parts on the earth, in air space, or in outer space, including the Moon and other celestial bodies.

These Articles lay down three principles of which two at least are novel. The first is the international responsibility of a State for space operations conducted as non-governmental enterprises or private persons; the second is the joint and several responsibility of an international organization and its participating member States for space operations in which it engages. The third is an extension of international law in that joint liability for damage caused is incurred by the State launching a spacecraft, a State procuring its launching, and the State from whose territory it is launched, where they are different.

On the assumption that space operations are on too large and public a scale for them to be undertaken from the territory of a State without its participation or consent, the State will either have contracted out the whole or part of the operation to a non-governmental enterprise or it will have licensed its conduct by the enterprise. But it is not clear from Articles 6 and 7 whether 'national activities', for which the State is responsible under Article 6, means activities of its nationals or only activities within its territorial jurisdiction: in other words, if a non-governmental enterprise seeks to enter into an agreement with another State to conduct space operations in its territory, will the State of its nationality be responsible for those operations on the principle of continuing supervision? The authorization or licensing of space-operations by non-governmental enterprises must in any event be matter for domestic legislation.

The principle of the joint and several responsibility of an international organization and of its Member States for space operations in which it engages, raises some curious questions. The principle as it appears in Resolution 1962–XVIII, paragraph 5, is inevitably modified when it is taken into the Treaty because its application is no longer general but is limited to the States parties. We may then ask how an international organization can, as a separate international person, be bound to observe the provisions of a treaty, to which it is not a party and to which it cannot, without amendment of the treaty, become a party. It is to be noted that in any case an international organization is not liable under the terms of the Outer Space Treaty for damage caused by its space operations.

This question may be avoided in practice where the majority of Member States, making the decisions of the organization on the conduct of space operations by it, are also parties to the Outer Space Treaty, and may be expected to adjust those decisions to its terms;[1] they could, in particular, be described as states 'procuring' the launching, for the purposes of Article 7.

But the question still remains whether what appears to be a principle of *several* responsibility of members of an international organization for its acts and decisions is not new. Article 13(2) may have some bearing on this question. It provides:

> Any practical questions arising in connexion with activities carried on by international intergovernmental organizations in the exploration and use of outer space, including the Moon and other celestial bodies, shall be resolved by the States parties to the Treaty either with the appropriate international organization or with one or more State members of that international organization which are parties to this Treaty.

I do not want to explore all the obscurities of this provision, which

[1] Article 13(1) makes the provisions of the Treaty applicable to space operations of States 'carried on within the framework of international intergovernmental organizations'.

is of doubtful legality as it stands, but it could, though I am far from certain about it, be saying something like this: situations may arise in the conduct of space operations by an international organization where States parties to the Treaty, which are members of it, may have to assume responsibility together for any disregard by the organization of the provisions of the Treaty.

That an international organization may be answerable for the consequences of its acts or decisions has been clearly established by the International Court. An organization has duties as well as rights,[1] and where its contractual obligations are cast in a liquidated sum it must pay it.[2] No reason appears why the position should be different in delict, or that the organization should not be under the general duty to make reparation for injury or harm done by it.

The extent of the obligations of members of an organization in these cases, that is their liability to be assessed for contribution or to contribute to any sums to be paid, must be determined by its constitutive instrument. But does the principle expressed in Article 6 of the Treaty render them severally liable to third parties for acts of the organization? In interpreting Article 17(2)[3] of the U.N. Charter, the International Court expressly declined to examine the meaning of 'shall be borne', so that we have no guidance on whether the Court would hold members severally liable for expenses of the Organization, which it was unable or failed to pay.[4]

That there may be a place for a rule of limited liability was indicated by Judge Moreno Quintana dissenting in the same case:

> if all the Member States of the U.N. were obliged to bear burdens over and above the responsibility to which they had committed themselves, then the financial power of the organization would be substituted for the national powers of each of its Members.[5]

The character and scale of space operations requires that the new principle of individual responsibility of members of an organization, if indeed it is new, be clarified; that a rule of limited liability for members be introduced; and that in any case Article 13(2) be amended.

* * *

[1] *Reparation for Injuries Case*, loc. cit., on p. 6.

[2] *Awards of U.N. Administrative Tribunal* [1954] *ICJ Rep.*, 52.

[3] 'The expenses of the organization shall be borne by the Members as apportioned by the General Assembly.'

[4] *Certain Expenses of the U.N. Case* [1962] *ICJ Rep.*, 158. [5] Ibid., at 248.

It is indeed likely that the problems of management of space operations will lead to the development of new forms of international enterprise and responsibility, not least through the intrusion of commercial factors. Among legal forms of co-operation to be found at present in both international law and municipal law are contract, partnership and incorporation. Internationally they are created only by treaty; but where a treaty establishes a form of intergovernmental partnership or incorporates an international organization, it may directly or by analogy embody some of the institutions of municipal law. This may be shown in the field of space communications by a comparative study of the agreements concluded in 1964 for a global commercial communications system, and the agreement establishing the Société Européenne pour le Financement de Matériel Ferroviaire (EUROFIMA) in 1955.

It may be useful to turn aside here briefly to describe some of the forms and methods of space communications. Space communications may be commands given to a spacecraft for its direction or control, or observations made by it and telemetered back to Earth, or communications between spacecraft or stations, or telecommunications between points on the surface of the Earth using objects in orbit as the medium.

At least three kinds of object have been tried or used for telecommunications: the passive reflectors, of which the ECHO balloons and the orbiting copper needles, tried in the famous West Ford experiment, are examples, and the active instrumental Earth satellite, which now holds the field, and may act as a repeater or as a relay. So COURRIER I-B, designed for military use, and launched by the United States in October 1960, could receive and 'memorize' up to 280,000 words and repeat them as staged messages on command. EARLY BIRD, launched in April 1965, and SYNCOM, launched in January 1967, are pioneer satellites; each is able to relay communications on hundreds of channels, where even modernized submarine cables provide only scores, and is likely to have ever increasing development and use.

Important among the elements that must be taken into account in the design of space telecommunications systems are the number of channels that it is desired to put into use, and the requirements of what may be called the radio 'visibility' of satellites. The number of channels needed to provide telecommunications, other than television, in 1975 has been estimated, for example, for the Atlantic at 2100, the Americas at 1600 and for the Indian subcontinent at 660. The INTELSAT series to be launched in 1968 will each carry 1200 channels, representing about five times the capacity of EARLY BIRD. Whether extension[1] and economies in the use of submarine cables can compete with this remains to be seen. The radio 'visibility' of a satellite is determined partly by the altitude above the Earth of points in its orbit, and partly by its altitude above the horizon in respect of any given ground station; if the latter is less than about 8°, background noise will impair reception. An apogee altitude of a relay satellite of 1000 miles will give it radio 'visibility' for about seven minutes for two ground stations three thousand miles apart; an apogee altitude of 12,000 miles will provide 'visibility' for four hours or more.[2] Among possible systems then are either a large number of relay satellites in both equatorial and polar orbits, random or phased; or a small number in synchronous orbits at an altitude of about 22,300 miles. It is characteristic of these relay satellites, of which SYNCOM was the first, that they remain over a fixed point on the surface of the Earth, subject to small corrections for drift. Three synchronous satellites can together provide radio 'visibility' for the whole Earth.

The establishment of a space telecommunications system on commercial lines involves not only capital investment, risk and profit, but the participation of governments, since the necessary instruments are still largely in the hands of government agencies. Two linked agreements concluded in 1964, made 'interim arrangements providing for the establishment of a single global commercial communications satellite system', and designed 'to permit all States to have access to the global system and those States so wishing to invest in the system with consequent participation in the design, development, construction (including the provision of equipment), establishment, maintenance, operation and ownership of the system'.[3]

The Principal Agreement, to which over fifty governments are now

[1] SEACOM was established in 1961 linking Hong Kong, Singapore, Australia, New Guinea, and, at Guam, the United States–Japan cable.

[2] The Russian MOLNIYA III with capacity for about 1500 channels is of this type, and relayed, as a test, colour television between Moscow and Paris.

[3] Principal Agreement: Preamble, paras. 2, 4.

parties, lays down the main principles of participation in the system and its management and control. The Special Agreement, to which governments or designated telecommunications agencies may be parties,[1] provides for the necessary commercial and technical operations and from its participants an Interim Committee of management was formed. Both Agreements are open to accession by any member of ITU.[2]

The effective participants in the scheme are governments, the designated telecommunications agencies,[3] and 'communications carriers'. Ownership of the assets of the system is vested in the parties to the Special Agreement, thus:

> The space segment shall be owned in undivided shares by the signatories to the Special Agreement in proportion to their respective contributions to the costs of the design, development, construction and establishment of the space segment.[4]

The 'space segment' comprises

> the communications satellite and the tracking, control, command and related facilities and equipment required to support the operation of the communications satellites.[5]

The Interim Communications Satellite Committee (Intelcom) is given

> responsibility for the design, development, construction, establishment, maintenance and operation of the space segment of the system.[6]

on the bases, first that

> administrations and communications will, subject to the requirements of their applicable domestic law, negotiate and enter directly into such traffic agreements as may be appropriate . . .[7]

second, that

> no Earth station shall be permitted to utilize the space segment unless it has been approved by the Special Committee . . .[8]

and thirdly, that COMSAT shall

> pursuant to general policies of the Committee, and in accordance with

[1] Article II*a*: 'Each party either shall sign or shall designate a communications entity, public or private, to sign the Special Agreement.' [2] Article IX*b*(ii).

[3] In some cases there are the postal and telecommunications administrations, and occasionally statutory corporations (COMSAT) or private corporations (Kokusai Denshin Denwa Co. Ltd, Japan).

[4] Article III. [5] Article I*b*(i). [6] Article IV*a*.

[7] Article II*b*: among matters to be agreed are: the use of communications channels provided by the system; services to be furnished to the public; divisions of revenue, and other commercial arrangements. [8] Article VII.

specific determinations which may be made by the Committee, act as manager . . .[1]

Some general comments may be offered on these intricate arrangements. First, the idea of a corporate body like EUROFIMA, is for the time being at least rejected,[2] and there is established what is in effect a commercial partnership or consortium between governments and telecommunications agencies. Given that the responsibility of a government for such an agency, designated by it to be a party to the Special Agreement, must be governed by domestic law[3] and that, even where it is a private enterprise, the government will be internationally responsible for it under Outer Space Treaty, Article 6, there appears to be no practical distinction between governments and telecommunications agencies as participants in the scheme.

It is clear that the International Satellite Telecommunications Consortium is not at present an international organization, in the sense of being an international legal person. It is expressly described as an interim arrangement, and even if it were an international organization it is uncertain whether it would be intergovernmental in the sense of Article 13 of the Outer Space Treaty.

Second, ownership of the space segment is vested in the participants in proportion to their respective contributions, though it is not then clear what is meant by saying that the ownership is in undivided shares, a phrase oddly reminiscent of our land law before 1925. In the case of EUROFIMA, a company incorporated in Switzerland with some necessary modifications of the applicable Swiss law, what may be called by analogy the railway segment is vested in it, the participating railway companies being simply shareholders.

Third, financial contributions to the estimated cost of the space segment, which is U.S. $200 million, are assessed on a quota system,[4]

[1] Article VIII.

[2] Article IX*a* requires Intelsat to report not later than 1 January 1969, on whether the interim arrangements should be continued on a permanent basis or 'a permanent international organization, with a general conference and an international administrative and technical staff' should be established.

[3] So Article II*a*.

[4] The initial quotas in percentages were: United States 61; United Kingdom 8·4; France and Germany 6·1 each; Canada 3·75; Australia 2·75; Italy 2·2; Switzerland and Japan 2 each; the remaining participants, less than 1·5 each. It was agreed that new participants should be assessed up to a combined maximum of 17%, and existing contributions be then *pro tanto* reduced, but not so that the United States quota should be brought below 50·5%.

which is also the basis of representation in Intelcom and of voting rights in it, and recalls the quota system in use in the IMF and IBRD. But, since the quotas are directly related to the investment made, voting rights are proportional to the commercial risks undertaken, and therefore more realistic than those established in ITU on the basis of old prestige rather than current interest. The enormous preponderance of the United States vote is only slightly reduced by the requirement of qualified majorities for decisions on such matters as the general standards to be laid down for access by Earth stations to satellites, the placing of contracts in the space segment, and the fixing of rates to be charged; but Intelcom will no doubt in practice seek unanimity of decision, as the Special Agreement proposes.

Fourth, the construction, management and use of the system are not only global in extent and based on the principle of non-discrimination, but involve several disparate kinds of legal arrangement: traffic agreements between administrations and communications carriers; the placing of contracts by Intelcom for the design, construction and maintenance of the system, such contracts being presumably concluded with COMSAT; licences by Intelcom for access to and use of the system; and leases of channels by administrations or communications carriers, which are not parties to the Special Agreement. Further, the relationship of the whole arrangement to ITU, at some aspects of which I shall look later, is still being worked out. It is perhaps not surprising that the simple pattern of EUROFIMA was not followed, by which railway materials and equipment are purchased by EUROFIMA, and rented to the participating railway companies on what is essentially a hire-purchase arrangement, protected by governmental guarantees.

We have then a new kind of international commercial partnership. It is larger in scale and potentiality than EUROFIMA and more flexible; but its legal features are not so sharply delineated, and, more important perhaps, there is less international control in the full sense. For Intelsat is an arrangement designed to make room for both public and private enterprise. The Communications Satellite Act 1962, which established COMSAT, bluntly asserts the claims of private enterprise in s.102(*c*)

In order to facilitate this development and to provide for the widest possible participation by private enterprise, United States participation in the global system shall be in the form of a private corporation, subject to appropriate governmental regulation. It is the intent of Congress that all authorized users shall have non-discriminatory access to the system; that the corporation created under this Act be so organized and operated as to maintain and strengthen competition in the provision of communications services to the public and that the activities of the corporation . . . and of the persons or companies participating in [its] ownership[1] . . . shall be consistent with the Federal anti-trust laws.

Special content is then given to the rule in Resolution 1962–XVIII and Outer Space Treaty, Article 1(2), that access to and use of outer space shall be free and without discrimination. Under Article 6 of the Treaty States are to be internationally responsible for the activities of non-governmental enterprises, and this is supported, in so far as they are telecommunications agencies, by the requirement in Article II*b* of the Principal Agreement of 1964 that their relations with governments shall be subject to the particular domestic law. It follows at least for States that are parties to both instruments,[2] first that the principles of free competition and the elimination of restrictive trade practices must be observed in the establishment and operation of the space telecommunications system, and second, that there is an obligation to bring domestic law into conformity with those principles, where that is necessary. Indeed since COMSAT is at present manager of the INTELSAT system and is subject as such to Federal anti-trust laws, there could be conflicts if Intelcom pursued policies deviating from these principles.

But it remains to be seen how these principles will be applied. A new consortium, called World Satellite Terminals, has already evolved a standard design of ground station 'dishes', with a chance of capturing the market. COMSAT itself has claimed priority over the American Broadcasting Corporation for the operation of television relay by satellite, and the use of the same satellite or group of satellites for both governmental and commercial purposes might yield privileges to the private users; thus the NASCOM/Apollo Satellites, to be used for communications in the landing of a manned space-

[1] Of the 10 million $20 shares of common stock, one-half are held by communications common carriers and one-half by the general public.

[2] The Soviet Union declined participation in the Agreements of 1964, but agreed to reserve enough radio frequencies to serve space communications needs for the next twenty years: *Keesing's Archives* 20614.

craft on the Moon, are expected to have a considerable number of spare channels for commercial use.[1]

The first annual report of the Comsat Corporation[2] stresses its competitive difficulties. Pointing out that 'internationally our position rests on temporary agreements among governments and telecommunications entities', the report expects the domestic communications satellite system to provide a larger market than the international over the next decade; and it appears that EARLY BIRD has so far been operated at a loss. But the report points out that 'the development of satellite services must in a number of places proceed in competition with established financial and political interests in cables and other terrestrial lines'.

There are analogies here with the problems of competition and monopoly arising in the European Economic Community, and their solution in an international framework under Articles 85 and 86 of the Rome Treaty, which established the Community. COMSAT, as we have seen, is also faced with competitors outside the system established by the 1964 Agreements.[3] A Supplementary Agreement on Arbitration, annexed to the Special Agreement, makes provision for the settlement of disputes in the field of telecommunications. The Court of Arbitration of the International Chamber of Commerce might also be a suitable forum, particularly since it has had much experience of commercial disputes involving both governments and private enterprises.

The European Space Research Organization (ESRO) was established in Paris in 1964 'to provide for and to promote collaboration among European states in space research and technology'. It has ten members and a number of establishments: at Noordwijk for technology, at Darmstadt for data analysis, and at Frascati for research. It maintains a range for the launching of 'sondes' at Kruna, and telemetry stations in Alaska, Spitsbergen and the Falkland Islands. It, and its companion the European Launcher Development

[1] NAVSAT (Satellite Navigation Corporation) is similar. Designed to provide world-wide navigational aids by satellite for ships and aircraft, it will have three satellite 'arrays'—commercial, governmental, and reserve—in synchronous orbits.

[2] See *New Scientist* (6 April 1967), p. 17.

[3] This issue of outside competition with the European Communities was raised but not decided in *ASSIDER v. High Authority of the European Coal and Steel Community* [1955] *European Communities Court: Case* 5–55.

Organization, are the only regional organizations so far established for space activities.

In the field of space operations there are many bilateral agreements in addition to the global arrangements we have described. The United States agreed with the Soviet Union in 1962 on common meteorological and communications studies, and has arrangements with sixteen countries for the launching of 'sondes' and with ESRO for the launching of space probes, instrumented in Europe. France and the Soviet Union reached agreement in June 1966 for the launching of French space probes with Soviet launches.

The agreement between NASA in the United States and the U.S.S.R. Academy of Sciences, concluded in October 1965, provided for the exchange of meteorological data obtained from satellites and for the publication of a joint review on space biology and medicine. This agreement is of special significance, since it points once more to the fact that international co-operation in space activities is by no means only governmental or obtainable only through formal intergovernmental agreement. While both NASA and the U.S.S.R. Academy of Sciences may both be regarded, though in different senses, as State agencies, the agreement may be fairly described as being non-governmental and essentially within the field of activity of ICSU. The importance of ICSU as a centre of co-operation in the exploration and uses of outer space can hardly be overestimated, its effectiveness being the greater through its freedom from some of the inhibitions that must attend the collaboration of governments; and the provisions for consultation in the Outer Space Treaty, and in particular Article 9, must be understood, as was formally stated by the United States Government, as meaning consultation through ICSU and its special committee on space research (COSPAR).

* * *

A particular problem of the organization of space activities, which calls for attention because it has been considered by the Legal Sub-committee of CPUOS[1] and is dealt with in the Outer Space Treaty, is that of assistance to astronauts, and the recovery of them and their spacecraft, in an emergency. Article 5 of the Treaty provides that:

[1] See U.N. Doc. A/A.105/29 (1.10.1965). Further discussion was deferred in September 1966.

(1) States parties to the Treaty shall regard astronauts as envoys of mankind in outer space and shall render to them all possible assistance in the event of accident, distress or emergency landing on the territory of another State party or on the high seas. When astronauts make such a landing, they shall be safely and promptly returned to the State of registry of the space vehicle.

(2) In carrying on activities in outer space and on celestial bodies, the astronauts of one State party shall render all possible assistance to the astronauts of other States parties.

The picturesque description of astronauts as envoys of mankind comes from Resolution 1962–XVIII, paragraph 9, which Article 5(1) repeats in substance, and it bears a faint impression of the idea of diplomatic immunity. But even without this it would be reasonable to suppose that under international law to be found in the customary rules of maritime distress and the Chicago Convention, Article 25,[1] astronauts, landing in emergency on foreign territory could not be regarded as unlawful entrants. But the question was posed in the Legal Subcommittee of the right of the State or international organization, launching the spacecraft concerned, to intervene, if necessary, on the territory of the foreign State to assist their astronauts. Such a right, reflecting perhaps the provisions of Article 25 of the Chicago Convention, must be taken to be excluded by implication from the Outer Space Treaty by the requirement that the astronauts in such a case must be safely and promptly returned. It would be artificial to treat Article 8(2) as an instance of a treaty creating rights and obligations for individuals: it is rather a declaration of the demands of common humanity that must in their nature be made and answered between individuals.

The right of recovery of a spacecraft, or its component parts, which have landed in the territory of a foreign state, has been questioned. It has for example been said that according to existing international law, a sovereign State has a complete and exclusive jurisdiction within the limits of its territory; so that 'a spacecraft . . . landed on the territory of another State is placed under its jurisdiction and the launching State has no legal basis for demanding its return save

[1] But see McDougal, Lasswell and Vlasic, *Law and Public Order in Space*, op. cit., at 269, for the view that Article 25 may be confined to cases of authorized entry.

under a bilateral or multilateral agreement to this effect.'[1] The provisions of Article 8 of the Treaty settle the point, since ownership of the spacecraft and its component parts continues up to and after its return to Earth; and secondly

Such objects or component parts found beyond the limits of the State party to the Treaty on whose registry they are carried shall be returned to that State, which shall upon request furnish identifying data prior to their return.

I shall turn finally to what must be the object of all organization, order in the uses of outer space.

[1] F. Ikeda, *Need for a Convention on the Rescue of Astronauts and Space Vehicles*, *International Symposium on Space Technology and Science* (Tokyo, 1962).

Chapter V

ORDER

IN order to try to describe elements of disorder in the uses of outer space, I shall use the closely linked concepts of damage, interference, waste and nuisance. While they are not mutually exclusive, since interference, waste and nuisance may cause damage, and persistent interference may amount to nuisance, these concepts can be distinguished in a number of ways: in the kinds of effects they are used to describe, in the lack of development of international law on interference, waste and nuisance as compared with damage;[1] and in the relative likelihood of their occurrence in the uses of outer space.

Damage could be taken to cover loss of life, injury to persons or property, and subject to exclusion for remoteness, consequential damage. In space operations damage may occur through accidents on the launching ground; through spacecraft, including launchers, or fragments of them, falling to the Earth; or through collisions between spacecraft and aircraft or between spacecraft themselves. Article 7 of the Outer Space Treaty makes operating States

> internationally liable for damage to another State party to the Treaty or to its natural or juridical persons by such object or its component parts on the Earth, in airspace, or in outer space, including the Moon and other celestial bodies.

Cast in the traditional form of international claims, this provision adds nothing to paragraph 8 of Resolution 1962–XVIII which it virtually reproduces. The Legal Subcommittee of CPUOS has still before it three sets of draft rules on liability for such damage, submitted by the United States, Belgium and Hungary.[2] It would not be useful here to list the points of disagreement between them, or to speculate on what conclusions of the Legal Subcommittee are likely or desirable.

[1] For an excellent study of the whole field see L. F. E. Goldie, 'Liability for Damage and International Law', 14 *ICLQ* [1965] 1188.

[2] For substantive texts see C. W. Jenks, *Space Law* (1965), 453–62.

However, there appears to be agreement on two central points, that the liability of the operating State shall be absolute for damage caused in the airspace or on the ground,[1] and that a claim in respect of damage shall be reduced or extinguished to the extent that it was contributed to or caused by the applicant State itself.[2] Of particular interest is the principle, which we have already discussed, that members of an international organization conducting space operations may be liable in certain circumstances for damage caused by it. This principle is adopted in both the United States and Hungarian drafts,[3] while the Belgian draft makes no mention of international organizations. The United States provision is more explicit than the Hungarian, making each member of the organization liable for compensation, in case of any default of payment by the organization of the sum duly awarded on the conditions that the member is a contracting party to the liability for damage Convention and that it shall not receive any payment in excess of the sum awarded. The Hungarian provision simply states that the financial obligations towards States suffering damage shall be met by the organization and its member States.

Liability for damage in outer space is not much elaborated and only the Hungarian draft gives it any precision. It is questionable whether the drafts as they stand would cover damage to stations or equipment on the Moon or other celestial bodies. The United States draft includes damage caused 'after the object has gone into orbit'; the Belgian draft speaks more vaguely of damage caused in 'the launching, motion or descent of all or part of the space device'; and the Hungarian draft refers simply to 'damage caused . . . in outer space' and defines a 'space object' as meaning 'spaceships, satellites, orbital laboratories, containers and any other devices designed for movement in outer space and sustained there otherwise than by reaction of air'. In short, the drafts appear to be at one in contemplating damage caused by and to spacecraft in orbit or, if beyond, then in movement. In the supposedly unlikely event of a collision between spacecraft, the United States and Belgian versions of the principle of absolute liability of the launching States would result it

[1] U.S. draft, Art. II(1); Belgian draft, Art. I(*b*); Hungarian draft, Art. VI.
[2] U.S. draft, Art. II(2); Belgian draft, Art. I(*c*); Hungarian draft, Art. VI.
[3] U.S. draft, Art. III(4); Hungarian draft, Art. VIII.

appears, in a claim and counterclaim, in which the damage suffered by each would be measured and the difference, if any, paid.

The Hungarian draft adopts the principle of absolute liability for damage caused in outer space only 'if the [launching] State is exercising an unlawful activity in outer space or the space vehicle or object has been launched for unlawful purposes'; otherwise there is liability for such damage only on proof of fault.[1]

On the crucial issue of the mode of presentation and settlement of claims for compensation, the Hungarian draft is defective and, as it appears to have the support of the Soviet Union, it does not augur well for the conclusion of an effective convention. The draft provides for the presentation of claims through diplomatic channels; but[2]

> 1. In case the State liable does not satisfy the claim of the damaged State, the claim for compensation shall be presented to a committee of arbitration on a basis of parity . . .
>
> 2. Should the committee . . . not arrive at a decision, the States may agree upon an international arbitration procedure, or any other method of settlement acceptable to both States.

This is not likely to commend itself as a satisfactory mode of settlement.

While damage caused by spacecraft or fragments of them after re-entry is likely to be infrequent, attribution of liability is not easy to establish. None of the drafts tackles the problem: the Belgian draft calls for 'proof . . . that there is a relationship of cause and effect between the damage . . . and the launching, motion or descent of all or part of the space device', and the Hungarian draft for 'evidence that damage has been caused', while the United States draft contains no express requirement of proof or evidence. But where fragments do not in some way identify themselves, what evidence can there be on which attribution of liability can be based, except an analysis of the detail of the launch, the flight elements, and the tracking record? The present public registry, maintained since 1962 by the United Nations under General Assembly Resolution 1721B–XVI, is neither complete nor uniform; and the COSPAR system of voluntary notification[3] of orbital elements or flight path and other information to assist tracking observations, being concerned with satellites and

[1] Articles IV and V.

[2] Article XII.

[3] For details see C. W. Jenks, *Space Law* (1965), 393–402.

space probes themselves, may not necessarily be a guide to the behaviour of the launchers; and it is mainly fragments of these that appear so far to have fallen to the Earth. In Article II of the Outer Space Treaty the States parties

> agree to inform the Secretary-General of the United Nations as well as the public and the international scientific community, to the greatest extent feasible and practicable, of the nature, conduct, locations and results . . .

of space operations. But if claims for damage are to be effectively made and satisfactorily settled, the existing arrangements for registration and notification of launchings and flight elements must be greatly improved.

* * *

The notion of interference caused by space operations would include the prevention of scientific observations or experiments, or serious impediments to them, and the creation of obstacles to space navigation. To demonstrate that scientific observations or experiments are being, or are likely to be impeded, and to control or avoid such interference, are problems for technical solution. Article 9 of the Outer Space Treaty, following paragraph 6 of Resolution 1962–XVIII, calls for international consultation where any State party, whether conducting a particular space operation or not,

> has reason to believe that an activity or experiment planned . . . in outer space, including the Moon and other celestial bodies, would cause potentially harmful interference with activities . . .

of other States in outer spaces; and also requires operating States to

> pursue studies in outer space, including the Moon and other celestial bodies and conduct exploration of them so as to avoid their harmful contamination.

These provisions are narrower than might have been expected for they do not seek to prohibit harmful interference with the environment of the Earth. However prior consultation, to be conducted as we have seen primarily through COSPAR and, where necessary, the specialized agencies, would go far to avoid impediments to research and other uses of outer space caused by careless action. Here I would recall that the objections raised by Sir Bernard Lovell to the West Ford experiment with orbiting copper needles in May 1961 were based, not upon an assured prediction that it would interfere with optical or radio astronomy, but upon the experiment having been unilaterally embarked on without proper consideration that it might so interfere. The fact that the orbiting dipoles were not found in the event to have disturbed astronomical observations does not in any way diminish the force of his argument.

* * *

COSPAR has laid down standards for the sterilization of space craft, designed for landing on the Moon or Mars, and certain principles of international order are beginning to crystallize around the ideas of waste and its opposite conservation, and of nuisance. Conservation is not the same as preservation for it aims not to prevent the use of resources, but to avoid waste now so as to ensure later use; nor is it the same as protection in a single interest, for it serves the common interest of all users. The first element is expressed in the Convention on Fishing and Conservation of the Living Resources of the High Seas 1966, Article 2, which defines conservation for the purposes of the Convention as

> the aggregate of the measures rendering possible the optimum sustainable yield from these resources.

The second element involves common rights and common obligations. So in the admittedly different context of international river navigation the Permanent Court described community of rights as

> the perfect equality of all riparian States in the use of the whole course of the river, and the exclusion of any preferential privilege of any one riparian State in relation to the others.[1]

The community of obligation is expressed in the opinion of the International Technical Conference on the Conservation of the Living Resources of the Sea 1955 that

> any effective conservation management system must have the participation of all States engaged in substantial exploitation of the stock or stocks of living marine organisms which are the object of the conservation management system or having a special interest in the conservation of that stock or stocks.[2]

[1] *Jurisdiction of the International Commission of the River Oder* [1929] *PCIJ: A* 23 at 27.

[2] Quoted in the U.N. Conference on the Law of the Sea 1958: Resolution on Co-operation in the Conservation Measures (25.4.1958): *Developments in the Law of the Sea* 1958–1964 (BIICL Special Publication No. 6), p. 39.

We might say then that conservation of natural resources must to be effective have two necessary elements: it must be designed to make possible the optimum sustainable yield over time, and there must be equality of participation of the users, both in their rights and their obligations.

Space operations present problems of conservation of the radio frequency spectrum and of the atmosphere. It may seem at first strange to apply the notion of conservation to the radio frequency spectrum, but it has been well said by an authority,[1] to whom I shall refer again, that

> it may be likened to an invisible natural resource uniformly distributed not merely for the Earth but throughout the Universe.

The radio frequency spectrum is not unlimited and the demands upon it multiply. Space communications not only make demands of their own, but offer the means for great expansion of Earth telecommunications and so increase the pressure on the spectrum. Nevertheless they bring also one countervailing benefit:

> the dimensions available for spectrum management are frequency, time and space. Frequency and time are unidimensional. Before the advent of space technology, 'space' as a dimension in spectrum management consisted for practical purposes of two coordinates, the latitude and longitude of a point on the Earth's surface. Space technology makes an available additional spatial dimension for frequency management: vertical distance from the Earth's surface. We now have five, instead of four variables, at our command for spectrum management.[2]

But the opportunity has not yet been taken to rationalize the use of radio frequencies. ITU regulation of them still falls short of satisfying the tests of conservation just suggested or of maintaining global order; and the deficiency is likely, in the absence of firm and comprehensive international arrangements, to be intensified by space communications. In the first place, while the ITU has made effective allocations of frequency bands to various services, the assignment of frequencies within those bands to particular stations has been left to domestic arrangement, either commercial or governmental, or at most regional agreement; so frequencies for sound and television

[1] J. H. Glazer, 'Infelix ITU: The Need for Space-age revisions', 23 *Federal Bar Journal* (Winter 1963).

[2] From brief filed by General Electric Co. with the Federal Communications Commission in March 1961, and quoted by J. H. Glazer, op. cit. at 24.

broadcasting in the European broadcasting area were distributed at conferences in 1948 and 1952, but a number of area countries remain outside the scheme. Secondly, not all States have adopted the regulations which form part of the ITU system,[1] and where they have, enforcement is again left to domestic action, there being no international sanction against breaches of them. Further there are no conditions or restrictions imposed upon the use of 'military radio installations' of ITU members.[2] The optimum use of the radio frequencies spectrum within a framework of probable future requirement is not then yet assured, nor do all users by any means participate in the ITU management system.

It would hardly be possible to extend the provisions of Article 9 of the Outer Space Treaty to cover in any effective way 'harmful interference' through use or abuse of radio frequencies. If, which is not obvious, the expression 'activity or experiment planned in outer space' is to be understood as including Earth-space communications auxiliary to the operation, there is no regulation of them in the Treaty.

Broadcasting by satellite may provoke trouble. Commercial or non-governmental broadcasting could pose problems similar to that by 'pirate' radio ships and installations; in a governmental form, it could have sharp political implications for many countries. The possibilities of commercial broadcasting are naturally complex. But, on the assumption that a State party to the Outer Space Treaty is responsible[3] for the broadcasting enterprise in the sense of Article 6, two observations may be made. First, commercial broadcasting by it by satellite would be an activity in outer space, requiring authorization and continuing supervision by the State, under that Article, regardless of the terrestrial point of origin of the broadcast. Secondly, where the State of nationality is not a member of the ITU but, as seems likely for some time to come, the broadcast has had to be made through the Intelsat system,[4] it is possible that Intelcom will subject

[1] For those devised for space communications see C. W. Jenks, *Space Law* (1965), Appendix IV.

[2] ITU Convention 1965, Article 50.

[3] The link appears to be nationality as determined by rules of private international law.

[4] See ITU Regulations, Section IIA, 84AP, defining a broadcasting satellite service as 'a space service in which signals transmitted, or retransmitted by reflection, from objects in orbit around the Earth, are intended for direct reception by the general public'.

approval for the broadcast under Article VII of the Principal Agreement to conditions and standards not less and, it might be hoped, more rigorous than those of the International Telecommunications Union.[1]

*   *   *

That the atmosphere of the Earth is a vital natural resource, and that its elements need conservation and protection from harmful interference, hardly needs saying. A Consultative Group of experts established by COSPAR, reported in May 1964 on the potentially harmful effects of space experiments.[2] It had considered three principal topics: pollution of the upper atmosphere, orbiting dipoles, and the contamination of the Moon and planets. It set at rest some of the earlier fears expressed about the possible injury to the upper atmosphere by the metallic vapours discharged by large rockets, but called for continuing experimental and theoretical studies. It said, in its conclusions about the upper atmosphere:

> The Consultative Group is aware of the dire consequences of contamination that have been cited in certain public pronouncements, and has examined them as far as present knowledge permit. (Examples of these are: the removal of the ozone layer, thereby permitting far-ultraviolet sunlight through to the ground; the removal of the free electrons in the ionosphere by introducing an electron 'getter' in large quantities; changing the temperature of the atmosphere by changing the water vapor or carbon dioxide content, etc.) We are unable to identify any physical processes which would produce these consequences. Although it is always possible that there might be other undesirable effects which have not been anticipated, this seems unlikely.

But it made, apart from the call for further 'serious quantitative studies', two reservations: that its study had been 'based on information in the open literature', and that it had not taken account of three contingencies that might be realized in the next few years: the use of nuclear-powered rockets and nuclear reactors in satellites, and the extensive use of high-flying supersonic transport aircraft or of disintegrating meteorological rockets.

The contingencies considered in the report, in so far as they might lead to pollution or major disturbance of the atmosphere, come as

[1] Compare ITU Radio Regulations, Art. 7(1) and 28(6), prohibiting broadcasting stations on 'ships, aircraft, or any other floating or airborne objects'.

[2] The report is reproduced in C. W. Jenks, *Space Law*, op. cit., 402–13 and in U.N. Doc. A/AC.105/20, Annex III.

much under the concepts of injury, and nuisance as of conservation; though nuisance may be too modest a word to describe nuclear tests in the upper atmosphere. The Nuclear Test Ban Treaty 1963 prohibits[1] such tests in the atmosphere or 'beyond the atmosphere including outer space', language designed, I believe, to prevent fine distinctions being made on the boundaries of the atmosphere. To these contingencies must be added the perhaps more remote contamination of the Earth by hostile micro-organisms from Mars or the subsoil of the Moon, which spacecraft must be prevented from bringing back from their explorations.[2]

These contingencies have been described in terms of abuse of rights, of a balancing of social damage and social utility, and of nuisance. The balancing of utility and damage can lead to a practical conclusion only within limited magnitudes. So in a contextual approach to the use of nuclear weapons Professor McDougal opposes to the 'disproportionate and unnecessary destruction of values' on the one hand, 'stringent necessity and much larger military advantage' on the other.[3] We may ask: To what is the destruction disproportionate and how can there be a real balancing when necessity is one of the terms? But the essential point is that here we have passed beyond the limits of practical reason: given the alternatives posed we may make a choice, but we cannot make a judgement.

The concept of nuisance has in this field certain advantages over the concepts of damage and abuse of rights: its generality and its flexibility. It is a concept of the common interest and public order; and radiation, pollution and contamination on a large geographical scale can be properly dealt with in terms only of public law and not of individual State rights based on private law analogies. Further, nuisance may cover danger to life, and injury to health of human beings and of the animals or plants, upon which their lives depend or which for other reasons need protection.

It has already had some recognition in international law in the contexts of air and water pollution and nuclear radiation; and in considering the instruments and decisions dealing with these we are not

[1] Article I(1)*a*.

[2] Outer Space Treaty, Article 9(2).

[3] McDougal and Feliciano, *Law and Minimum World Public Order* (Yale University Press, 1961), 663. See also McDougal and Schlei, 'The H-Bomb tests in perspective', 64 *Yale Law Journal* [1955] 691.

prevented from discerning the use of concept by the fact that it is not expressly named; for

the true view of the duty of international tribunals in this matter is to regard any features or terminology which are reminiscent of the rules and institutions of private law as an indication of policy and principles rather than as directly importing these rules and institutions.[1]

So the *Trail Smelter Award* was cast in terms, not so much of negligence or fault, but of strict liability for the use of territory injurious to neighbours; and in the *Lac Lanoux Arbitral Award* it was held that if the returned waters had

a chemical composition or a temperature or some other character which could injure Spain's interests

the claim would have been established.[2]

The High Seas Convention 1962, Article 25(2) calls for international co-operation for

the prevention of pollution of the seas or airspace above, resulting from any activities with radioactive materials or other harmful agents.

Similarly Article 24 requires States to draw up regulations

to prevent pollution of the seas by the discharge of oil from ships or pipelines or resulting from the exploitation and exploration of the seabed and its subsoil . . .

which serves to generalize provisions of the Convention for the Prevention of Pollution of the Sea by Oil 1954–1962. The provisions in a large number of river treaties aimed against pollution by industrial waste and other effluents were subsumed into the proposition of law in the *Lac Lanoux Arbitral Award* already quoted.

In applying the concept of nuisance to space operations, we may say that as a start Resolution 1963–XVIII should be implemented to achieve international agreement on three points: that the system of consultation and studies of the effects of space operations already instituted by COSPAR, should be expanded into regular reports to

[1] per Judge Sir Arnold McNair: *Status of South West Africa Case* [1950] *ICJ Rep.* at 148.

[2] *Trail Smelter Award* [1941] 3 *RIAA* 1905, 1063: 'No State has the right to use or permit the use of its territory in such a manner as to cause injury by fumes in or to the territory of another or to property or persons therein, when the case is of serious consequence and the injury is established by clear and convincing evidence.' *Lac Lanoux Arbitral Award* [1957] 12 *RIAA* 281.

the U.N. Committee on the Peaceful Uses of Outer Space; that large-scale changes[1] in the atmosphere are a matter, not only of inter-State claims, but of international public order; and that for the consequences of pollution or disturbance of the atmosphere there should be absolute liability in the operating State.

* * *

It may not be out of place to end these lectures by suggesting that the exploration and uses of outer space call international law back to its prime source in the law of nature. The law of nature is a general name for the principles that neither man, as an individual nor the State, as a Machiavellian prince, can be a law unto themselves; and that if man will understand and respect his natural framework he can advance, but that if he ignores it he will be destroyed—*naturam furca expellas, tamen usque recurret*. All law is a model, either of behaviour or of explanation. A statute or treaty is a model of conduct; the theories of gravitation of Newton and of Einstein are models of explanation. All models, and these four are no exception, have a common function of prediction; the more comprehensive the model, the greater the predictability of behaviour whether of human beings or the physical world.

Space law is then a fruitful and necessary extension of the international law model to give a larger place to the common interest as against the interests of sovereignties. But in helping to bring order into space operations and their infrastructure by creating models of conduct, international law is also indirectly serving the models of explanation; for the orbiting telescope and the radio astronomer, if their paths are kept clear, may before long show the way to decisive choices between possible cosmological models. Perhaps this is the most exciting prospect of all.

[1] See *Draft Principles on Changes in the Environment of the Earth*, David Davies Memorial Institute, 1964, which uses permanence, intensity or wide geographical extent as criteria of large-scale changes.

Appendix I

UNITED STATES: COMMUNICATIONS SATELLITE ACT 1962

SEC. 102

(a) The Congress hereby declares that it is the policy of the United States to establish, in conjunction and in co-operation with other countries, as expeditiously as practicable a commercial communications satellite system, as part of an improved global communications network, which will be responsive to public needs and national objectives, which will serve the communication needs of the United States and other countries, and which will contribute to world peace and understanding.

(b) The new and expanded telecommunication services are to be made available as promptly as possible and are to be extended to provide global coverage at the earliest practicable date. In effectuating this program, care and attention will be directed toward providing such services to economically less developed countries and areas as well as those more highly developed, toward efficient and economical use of the electromagnetic frequency spectrum, and toward the reflection of the benefits of this new technology in both quality of services and charges for such services.

(c) In order to facilitate this development and to provide for the widest possible participation by private enterprise, United States participation in the global system shall be in the form of a private corporation, subject to appropriate governmental regulation. It is the intent of Congress that all authorized users shall have nondiscriminatory access to the system. That maximum competition be maintained in the provision of equipment and services utilized by the system; that the corporation created under this Act be so organized and operated as to maintain and strengthen competition in the provision of communications services to the public; and that the activities of the corporation created under this Act and of the persons or companies participating in the ownership of the corporation shall be consistent with the Federal antitrust laws.

(d) It is not the intent of Congress by this Act to preclude the use of the communications satellite system for domestic communications services where consistent with the provisions of this Act nor to preclude the creation of additional communications satellite systems, if required to meet unique governmental needs or if otherwise required in the national interest.

Appendix II

GENERAL ASSEMBLY: DECLARATION OF LEGAL PRINCIPLES

GOVERNING THE ACTIVITIES OF STATES IN THE EXPLORATION AND USE OF OUTER SPACE, 1962 (XVIII)

The General Assembly,

Inspired by the great prospects opening up before mankind as a result of man's entry into outer space,

Recognizing the common interest of all mankind in the progress of the exploration and use of outer space for peaceful purposes,

Believing that the exploration and use of outer space should be carried on for the betterment of mankind and for the benefit of States irrespective of their degree of economic or scientific development,

Desiring to contribute to broad international co-operation in the scientific as well as in the legal aspects of exploration and use of outer space for peaceful purposes,

Believing that such co-operation will contribute to the development of mutual understanding and to the strengthening of friendly relations between nations and peoples,

Recalling its resolution 110 (II) of 3 November 1947, which condemned propaganda designed or likely to provoke or encourage any threat to the peace, breach of the peace, or act of aggression, and considering that the aforementioned resolution is applicable in outer space.

Taking into consideration its resolutions 1721 (XVI) of 20 December 1961 and 1802 (XVII) of 14 December 1962, adopted unanimously by the States Members of the United Nations,

Solemnly declares that in the exploration and use of outer space States should be guided by the following principles:

1. The exploration and use of outer space shall be carried on for the benefit and in the interests of all mankind.

2. Outer space and celestial bodies are free for exploration and use by all States on a basis of equality and in accordance with international law.

3. Outer space and celestial bodies are not subject to national appropriation by claim of sovereignty, by means of use or occupation, or by any other means.

4. The activities of States in the exploration and use of outer space shall be carried on in accordance with international law, including the Charter of the United Nations, in the interest of maintaining international peace and security and promoting international co-operation and understanding.

5. States bear international responsibility for national activities in outer space, whether carried on by governmental agencies or by non-governmental entities, and for assuring that national activities are carried on in conformity with the principles set forth in the present Declaration. The activities of non-governmental entities in outer space shall require authorization and continuing supervision by the State concerned. When activities are carried on in outer space by an international organization, responsibility for compliance with the principles set forth in the Declaration shall be borne by the international organization and by the States participating in it.

6. In the exploration and use of outer space, States shall be guided by the principle of co-operation and mutual assistance and shall conduct all their activities in outer space with due regard for the corresponding interests of other States. If a State has reason to believe that an outer space activity or experiment planned by it or its nationals would cause potentially harmful interference with activities of other States in the peaceful exploration and use of outer space, it shall undertake appropriate international consultations before proceeding with any such activity or experiment. A State which has reason to believe that an outer space activity or experiment planned by another State would cause potentially harmful interference with activities in the peaceful exploration and use of outer space may request consultation concerning the activity or experiment.

7. The State on whose registry an object launched into outer space is carried shall retain jurisdiction and control over such object, and any personnel thereon, while in outer space. Ownership of objects launched into outer space, and of their component parts, is not affected by their passage through outer space or by their return to the earth. Such objects or component parts found beyond the limits of the State of registry shall be returned to that State, which shall furnish identifying data upon request prior to return.

8. Each State which launches or procures the launching of an object into outer space, and each State from whose territory or facility an object is launched, is internationally liable for damage to a foreign State or to its natural or juridical persons by such object or its component parts on the earth, in air space, or in outer space.

9. States shall regard astronauts as envoys of mankind in outer space, and shall render to them all possible assistance in the event of accident, distress, or emergency landing on the territory of a foreign State or on the high seas. Astronauts who make such a landing shall be safely and promptly returned to the State of registry of their space vehicle.

1280th plenary meeting,
13th December 1963

Appendix III

GENERAL ASSEMBLY: INTERNATIONAL CO-OPERATION IN THE PEACEFUL USES OF OUTER SPACE, 1963 (XVIII)

The General Assembly

Recalling its resolutions 1721 (XVI) of 20 December 1961 and 1802 (XVII) of 14 December 1962 on international co-operation in the peaceful uses of outer space,

Having considered the report submitted by the Committee on the Peaceful Uses of Outer Space,

Mindful of the benefits which all Member States would enjoy by participation in international programmes of co-operation in this field,

I

1. *Recommends* that consideration should be given to incorporating in international agreement form, in the future as appropriate, legal principles governing the activities of States in the exploration and use of outer space;

2. *Requests* the Committee on the Peaceful Uses of Outer Space to continue to study and report on legal problems which may arise in the exploration and use of outer space, and in particular to arrange for the prompt preparation of draft international agreements on liability for damage caused by objects launched into outer space and on assistance to and return of astronauts and space vehicles;

3. *Further Requests* the Committee on the Peaceful Uses of Outer Space to report to the General Assembly at its nineteenth session on the results achieved in preparing these two agreements;

II–IV

(deal with future work of CPUOS, WMO and ITU)

Appendix IV

AGREEMENT ESTABLISHING INTERIM ARRANGEMENTS FOR A GLOBAL COMMERCIAL COMMUNICATIONS SATELLITE SYSTEM

The Governments signatory to this Agreement, *recalling* the principle set forth in Resolution No. 1721 (XVI) of the General Assembly of the United Nations that communications by means of satellites should be available to the nations of the world as soon as practicable on a global and non-discriminatory basis;

Desiring to establish a single global commercial communications satellite system as part of an improved global communications network which will provide expanded telecommunications services to all areas of the world and which will contribute to world peace and understanding;

Determined, to this end, to provide, through the most advanced technology available, for the benefit of all nations of the world, the most efficient and economical service possible consistent with the best and most equitable use of the radio spectrum;

Believing that satellite communications should be organized in such a way as to permit all States to have access to the global system and those States so wishing to invest in the system with consequent participation in the design, development, construction (including the provision of equipment), establishment, maintenance, operation and ownership of the system;

Believing that it is desirable to conclude interim arrangements providing for the establishment of a single global commercial communications satellite system at the earliest practicable date, pending the working out of definitive arrangements for the organization of such a system;

Agree as follows:

Article I

(a) The Parties to this Agreement shall co-operate to provide, in accordance with the principles set forth in the Preamble to this Agreement, for the design, development, construction, establishment, maintenance and operation of the space segment of the global commercial communications satellite system, to include

(i) an experimental and operational phase in which it is proposed to use one or more satellites to be placed in synchronous orbit in 1965;

(ii) succeeding phases employing satellites, of types to be determined, with the objective of achieving basic global coverage in the latter part of 1967; and

(iii) such improvements and extensions thereof as the Committee established by Article IV of this Agreement may decide subject to the provisions of Article VI of this Agreement.

(b) In this Agreement,

(i) the term 'space segment' comprises the communications satellites and the tracking, control, command and related facilities and equipment required to support the operation of the communications satellites;

(ii) the terms 'design' and 'development' include research.

Article II

(a) Each party either shall sign or shall designate a communications entity public or private, to sign the Special Agreement which is to be concluded further to this Agreement and which is to be opened for signature at the same time as this Agreement. Relations between any such designated entity and the Party which has designated it shall be governed by the applicable domestic law.

(b) The Parties to this Agreement contemplate that administrations and communications carriers will, subject to the requirements of their applicable domestic law, negotiate and enter directly into such traffic agreements as may be appropriate with respect to their use of channels of communication provided by the system to be established under this Agreement, services to be furnished to the public, facilities, divisions of revenues and related business arrangements.

Article III

The space segment shall be owned in undivided shares by the signatories to the Special Agreement in proportion to their respective contributions to the costs of the design, development, construction and establishment of the space segment.

Article IV

(a) An Interim Communications Satellite Committee, hereinafter referred to as 'The Committee', is hereby established to give effect to the co-operation provided for by Article I of this Agreement. The Committee shall have responsibility for the design, development, construction, establishment, maintenance and operation of the space segment of the system and, in particular, shall exercise the functions and have the powers set forth in this Agreement and in the Special Agreement.

(b) The Committee shall be composed as follows: one representative from each of the signatories to the Special Agreement whose quota is not less than 1·5%, and one representative from any two or more signatories to the Special Agreement whose combined quotas total not less than 1·5% and which have agreed to be so represented.

(c) In the performance of its financial functions under this Agreement and under the Special Agreement the Committee shall be assisted by an advisory sub-committee on finance. This sub-committee shall be established by the Committee as soon as the Committee becomes operative.

(d) The Committee may establish such other advisory sub-committees as it thinks fit.

(e) No signatory or group of signatories to the Special Agreement shall be deprived of representation on the Committee because of any reduction pursuant to Article XII (c) of this Agreement.
(f) In this Agreement, the term 'quota' in relation to a signatory to the Special Agreement, means the percentage set forth opposite its name in the Annex to the Special Agreement as modified pursuant to this Agreement and the Special Agreement.

Article V

a) Each signatory to the Special Agreement or group or signatories to the Special Agreement represented on the Committee shall have a number of votes equal to its quota, or to their combined quotas, as the case may be.
(b) A quorum for any meeting of the Committee shall consist of representatives having, in total, a number of votes exceeding the vote of the representative with the largest vote by not less than 8.5.
(c) The Committee shall endeavour to act unanimously; however, if it fails to reach agreement it shall take decisions by a majority of the votes cast, except that, with respect to the following matters, and subject to paragraphs (d) and (e) of this Article, any decisions must have the concurrence of representatives whose total votes exceed the vote of the representative with the largest vote by not less than 12.5:

(i) choice of type or types of space segment to be established;
(ii) establishment of general standards for approval of earth stations for access to the space segment;
(iii) approval of budgets by major categories;
(iv) adjustment of accounts pursuant to Article 4 (c) of the Special Agreement;
(v) establishment of the rate of charge per unit of satellite utilization pursuant to Article 9 (a) of the Special Agreement;
(vi) decisions on additional contributions pursuant to Article VI (b) of this Agreement;
(vii) approval of the placing of contracts pursuant to Article 10 (c) of the Special Agreement;
(viii) approval of matters relating to satellite launchings pursuant to Article 10 (d) of the Special Agreement;
(ix) approval of quotas pursuant to Article XII (a) (ii) of this Agreement;
(x) determination of financial conditions of accession pursuant to Article XII (b) of this Agreement;
(xi) decisions relating to withdrawal pursuant to Article XI (a) and (b) of this Agreement and Article 4 (d) of the Special Agreement;
(xii) recommendation of amendments pursuant to Article 15 of the Special Agreement;
(xiii) adoption of the rules of procedure of the Committee and the advisory sub-committees;
(xiv) approval of appropriate compensation to the Corporation for its performance of services as manager pursuant to Articles 5 (c) and 9 (b) of the Special Agreement.

(d) If the Committee, upon the expiration of sixty days following the date when such matter has been proposed for decision, shall not have taken a decision pursuant to paragraph (c) (i) of this Article on the type of space segment to be established to achieve the objective stated in paragraph (a) (ii) of Article I of this Agreement, a decision on such matter may thereafter be taken by the concurring votes of representatives whose total votes exceed the vote of the representative with the largest vote by not less than 8.5.

(e) If the Committee, upon the expiration of sixty days following the date when such matter has been proposed for decision, shall not have approved

(i) any particular budget category, pursuant to paragraph (c) (iii) of this Article,

(ii) the placing of any particular contract, pursuant to paragraph (c) (vii) of this Article, or

(iii) any particular matter relating to satellite launchings, pursuant to paragraph (c) (viii) of this Article, relating to achievement of the objectives stated in paragraphs (a) (i) and (a) (ii) of Article I of this Agreement, a decision on such matter may thereafter be taken by the concurring votes of representatives whose total votes exceed the vote of the representative with the largest vote by not less than 8.5.

Article VI

(a) The contributions of the signatories to the Special Agreement towards the costs of the design, development, construction and establishment of the space segment during the interim arrangements shall be based upon an estimate of U.S. $200,000,000 for such costs. Each signatory to the Special Agreement shall pay its quota of such costs in accordance with the provisions of the Special Agreement.

Article VII

In order to ensure the most effective utilization of the space segment in accordance with the principles set forth in the Preamble to this Agreement, no earth station shall be permitted to utilize the space segment unless it has been approved by the Committee pursuant to Article 7 of the Special Agreement.

Article VIII

The Communications Satellite Corporation, incorporated under the laws of the District of Columbia (herein referred to as the Corporation) shall, pursuant to general policies of the Committee and in accordance with specific determinations which may be made by the Committee, act as the manager in the design, development, construction, establishment, operation and maintenance of the space segment.

Article IX

(a) Having regard to the program outlined in Article I of this Agreement, within one year after the initial global system becomes operational and in any case not later than 1st January 1969, the Committee shall render a report to each Party to this Agreement containing the Committee's recommendations concerning the definitive arrangements for an international global system which shall supersede the interim arrangements established by this Agreement. This report, which shall be fully representative of all shades or opinion, shall consider, among other things, whether the interim arrangements should be continued on a permanent basis or whether a permanent international organization with a General Conference and an international administrative and technical staff should be established.

(b) Regardless of the form of the definitive arrangements,

(i) their aims shall be consonant with the principles set forth in the Preamble of this Agreement;

(ii) they shall, like this Agreement, be open to all States members of the International Telecommunication Union or their designated entities;

(iii) they shall safeguard the investment made by signatories of the Special Agreement; and

(iv) they shall be such that all parties to the definitive arrangements may have an opportunity of contributing to the determination of general policy.

(c) The report of the Committee shall be considered at an international conference, at which duly designated communications entities may also participate, to be convened by the Government of the United States of America for that purpose within three months following submission of the report. The Parties to this Agreement shall seek to ensure that the definitive arrangements will be established at the earliest practicable date, with a view to their entry into force by 1st January 1970.

Article X

In considering contracts and in exercising their other responsibilities, the Committee and the Corporation as manager shall be guided by the need to design, develop and procure the best equipment and services at the best price for the most efficient conduct and operation of the space segment. When proposals or tenders are determined to be comparable in terms of quality, c.i.f. price and timely performance, the Committee and the Corporation as manager shall also seek to ensure that contracts are so distributed that equipment is designed, developed and procured in the States whose Governments are Parties to this Agreement in approximate proportion to the respective quotas of their corresponding signatories to the Special Agreement; provided that such design, development and procurement are not contrary to the joint interests of the Parties to this Agreement and the signatories to the Special Agreement. The Committee and the Corporation as manager shall also seek to ensure that the foregoing principles are applied with respect to major sub-contracts to the extent that this can be accomplished without impairing the responsibility of the prime contractor for the performance of work under the contract.

Article XIV

Upon entry into force of this Agreement, the Government of the United States of America shall register it with the Secretary-General of the United Nations in accordance with Article 102 of the Charter of the U.N.

Article XV

This Agreement shall remain in effect until the entry into force of the definitive arrangements referred to in Article IX of this Agreement.

Appendix V

SPECIAL AGREEMENT

Whereas certain Governments have become Parties to an Agreement Establishing Interim Arrangements for a Global Commercial Communications Satellite System; and

Whereas those Governments have undertaken therein to sign or to designate a communications entity to sign this Special Agreement;

The signatories to this Special Agreement hereby agree as follows:

Article 1

In this Special Agreement:

(a) 'The Agreement' means the Agreement Establishing Interim Arrangements for a Global Commercial Communications Satellite System opened for signature on 20 August 1964, at Washington;

(b) 'The Committee' means the Interim Communications Satellite Committee established by Article IV of the Agreement;

(c) 'The Corporation' means the Communications Satellite Corporation incorporated under the laws of the District of Columbia pursuant to the Communications Satellite Act of 1962[1] of the United States of America;

(d) 'Design' and 'development' include research;

(e) 'Quota', in relation to a signatory, means the percentage set forth opposite its name in the Annex to this Special Agreement as modified pursuant to the Agreement and this Special Agreement;

(f) 'Signatory' means a Government or a communications entity which has signed this Special Agreement and in respect of which it is in force;

(g) 'The space segment' means the space segment defined in Article I (b) (i) of the Agreement.

Article 2

Each signatory undertakes to fulfil the obligations placed upon it by the Agreement and thereby obtains the rights provided therein.

Article 3

Each signatory undertakes to contribute a percentage of the costs of the design, development, construction and establishment of the space segment equal to its quota.

Article 4

(a) During a period of nine months from the date when the Agreement is first opened for signature, each signatory shall, within four weeks from

[1] 76 Stat. 423; 47 U.S.C. Sections 731–35.

the date of entry into force of this Special Agreement for that signatory, make a payment on account to the Corporation, in United States dollars, or in currency freely convertible into United States dollars, of a percentage equal to its quota of the expenditure which the Corporation has incurred for the design, development, construction and establishment of the space segment prior to the date when the Agreement is first opened for signature, and, according to estimates established by the Corporation at that date, is to incur for those purposes within six months after that date, together with its proportionate share of any additional contribution required pursuant to paragraph (b) of this Article, and appropriate interest on all such amounts. Each signatory shall pay the remainder of its contribution pursuant to Article 3 of this Special Agreement in accordance with paragraph (b) of this Article.

(b) The Corporation shall submit to the Committee estimates of the time phasing of payments required pursuant to Article 3 of this Special Agreement. The Committee shall call on the signatories to make their respective proportionate payments in order to enable obligations to be met as they become due. Payments shall be made to the Corporation by each signatory in United States dollars, or in currency freely convertible into United States dollars, and in such amounts that, accounting on a cumulative basis, the sums paid by the signatories are in proportion to their respective quotas. Where a signatory other than the Corporation incurs obligations pursuant to authorization by the Committee, the Committee shall cause payments to be made to that signatory.

(c) Accounts for expenditure referred to in paragraphs (a) and (b) of this Article shall be subject to review by the Committee and shall be subject to such adjustment as the Committee may decide.

(d) Each signatory shall pay the amount due from it under paragraph (b) of this Article on the date designated by the Committee. Interest at the rate of six per cent per annum shall be added to any amount unpaid after that date. If the signatory has not made a payment within three months of its becoming due, the rights of the signatory under the Agreement and this Special Agreement shall be suspended. If, after such suspension, the Committee decides, pursuant to Article XI (b) of the Agreement, that the defaulting signatory is deemed to have withdrawn from this Special Agreement, the Committee shall then make a binding determination of the sums already due together with a sum to be paid in respect of the costs which will result in the future from contracts concluded while that signatory was a party. Such withdrawal shall not, however, affect the obligation of the signatory concerned to pay sums due under this Special Agreement, whether falling due before it ceased to be a party or payable in accordance with the aforesaid determination of the Committee.

Article 5

The following shall be included as part of the costs of the design, development, construction and establishment of the space segment to be shared by the signatories in proportion to their respective quotas:

(a) The direct and indirect costs for the design, development, construction and establishment of the space segment incurred by the Corporation prior to the date when the Agreement is first opened for signature;

(b) All direct and indirect costs for the design, development, construction and establishment of the space segment incurred by the Corporation or pursuant to authorization by the Committee by any other signatory on behalf of the signatories to this Special Agreement subsequent to the date when the Agreement is first opened for signature;

(c) All direct and indirect costs incurred by the Corporation which are allocable to its performance of services as manager in the design, development, construction and establishment of the space segment and appropriate compensation to the Corporation, as may be agreed between the Corporation and the Committee, for such services.

Article 6

The following shall not form part of the costs to be shared by the signatories:

(a) Taxes on the net income of any of the signatories;

(b) Design and development expenditure on launchers and launching facilities except expenditure incurred for the adaptation of launchers and launching facilities in connection with the design, development, construction and establishment of the space segment;

(c) The costs of the representatives of the signatories on the Committee and on its advisory sub-committees and the staffs of those representatives except insofar as the Committee may otherwise determine.

Article 7

(a) In considering whether an earth station should be permitted to utilize the space segment, the Committee shall take into account the technical characteristics of the station, the technical limitations on multiple access to satellites due to the existing state of the art, the effect of geographical distribution of earth stations on the efficiency of the services to be provided by the system, the recommended standards of the International Telegraph and Telephone Consultative Committee and the International Radio Consultative Committee of the International Telecommunication Union, and such general standards as the Committee may establish. Failure by the Committee to establish general standards shall not of itself preclude the Committee from considering or acting upon any application for approval of an earth station to utilize the space segment.

(b) Any application for approval of an earth station to utilize the space segment shall be submitted to the Committee by the signatory to this Special Agreement in whose area the earth station is or will be located or, with respect to other areas, by a duly authorized communications entity. Each such application shall be submitted either individually or jointly on behalf of all signatories and duly authorized communications entities intending to utilize the space segment by means of the earth station which is the subject of the application.

(c) Any application for approval of an earth station located in the territory of a State whose Government is party to the Agreement which is to be owned or operated by an organization or organizations other than the corresponding signatory shall be made by that signatory.

Article 8

(a) Each applicant for approval of an earth station pursuant to Article 7 of this Special Agreement shall be responsible for making equitable and non-discriminatory arrangements for the use of the earth station by all signatories or duly authorized communications entities intended to be served by the earth station individually or jointly with other earth stations.

(b) To the extent feasible the Committee shall allot to the respective signatory or duly authorized communications entity, for use by each earth station which has been approved pursuant to Article 7 of this Special Agreement, an amount of satellite utilization appropriate to satisfy the total communications capability requested on behalf of all signatories and duly authorized communications entities to be served by such earth station.

(c) In making allotments of satellite utilization the Committee shall give due consideration to the quotas of the signatories to be served by each earth station.

Article 9

(a) The Committee shall specify the unit of satellite utilization and from time to time shall establish the rate of charge per unit at a level which, as a general rule, shall be sufficient, on the basis of the estimated total use of the space segment, to cover amortization of the capital cost of the space segment, an adequate compensation for use of capital, and the estimated operating, maintenance and administration costs of the space segment.

(b) In establishing the unit rate of charge pursuant to paragraph (a) of this Article, the Committee shall include in the estimated operating, maintenance and administration costs of the space segment the estimated direct and indirect costs of the Corporation which are allocable to its performance of services as manager in the operation and maintenance of the space segment and appropriate compensation to the Corporation, as may be agreed between the Corporation and the Committee, for such services.

(c) The Committee shall arrange for the payment of charges for allotments of satellite utilization to be made quarterly to the Corporation. The charges shall be computed in United States dollars and paid in United States dollars or in currency freely convertible into United States dollars.

(d) The components of the unit rate of charge representing amortization and compensation for the use of capital shall be credited to the signatories in proportion to their respective quotas. In the interests of avoiding unnecessary transfers of funds between signatories, and of keeping to a minimum the funds held by the Corporation on behalf of the signatories, the Committee shall make suitable arrangements for funds representing these components to be retained by signatories where appropriate or, if collected, to be distributed among the signatories in such a way that the credits established for signatories are discharged.

(e) The other components of the unit rate of charge shall be applied to meet all operating, maintenance, and administration costs, and to establish such reserves as the Committee may determine to be necessary. After providing for such costs and reserves, any balance remaining shall be distributed by the Corporation, in United States dollars, or in currency freely convertible into United States dollars, among the signatories in proportion to their respective quotas; but if insufficient funds remain to meet the operating, maintenance and administration costs, the signatories shall pay to the Corporation, in proportion to their respective quotas, such amounts as may be determined by the Committee to be required to meet the deficiency.

(f) The Committee shall institute appropriate sanctions in cases where payments pursuant to this Article shall have been in default for three months or longer.

Article 10

(a) All contracts placed by the Corporation or by any other signatory pursuant to authorization by the Committee relating to design, development and procurement of equipment for the space segment shall, except as otherwise provided by the Committee, be based on responses to appropriate requests for quotations or invitations to tender from among persons and organizations qualified to perform the work under the proposed contract whose names are furnished to the Committee by the signatories.

(b) For contracts which exceed U.S. $125,000 the issue by the Corporation of requests for quotations or invitations to tender shall be in accordance with such conditions as the committee may determine. The Corporation shall keep the Committee fully informed of decisions taken relating to such contracts.

(c) The Corporation shall consult the Committee before issuing requests for proposals and invitations to tender for contracts for design, development and procurement of equipment for the space segment which are expected to exceed U.S. $500,000. If, as a result of its evaluation of responses to such requests or invitations, the Corporation desires that a contract be placed which exceeds U.S. $500,000, it shall submit its evaluation and recommendations to the Committee. The approval of the Committee shall be required before each such contract is placed either by the Corporation as manager or by any other signatory pursuant to authorization by the Committee.

(d) The Committee shall approve the program for the launching of satellites and for associated services, the launch source and the contracting arrangements.

(e) Except as otherwise directed by the Committee, and subject to paragraphs (c) and (d) of this Article, all contractors shall be selected by the Corporation and all contracts shall be in the name of and be executed and administered by the Corporation as manager.

(f) Except as otherwise determined by the Committee, all contracts and sub-contracts placed for design, development and procurement of equipment for the space segment shall contain appropriate provisions to the effect that all inventions, technical data and information arising directly from any work performed under such contracts (except inventions, technical data and information pertaining to launchers and launchings) shall be disclosed to the Committee and may be used only in the design, development, manufacture and use of equipment and components for the space segment established under the present interim arrangements or under any definitive arrangements which may succeed these interim arrangements, without payment of royalties, by each signatory or any person in the jurisdiction of a signatory or the Government which has designated that signatory.

(g) Except as it may otherwise determine, the Committee shall endeavour to have included in all contracts placed for design and development appropriate provisions which will ensure that inventions, technical data and information owned by the contractor and its sub-contractors which are directly incorporated in work performed under such contracts, may be used on fair and reasonable terms by each signatory or any person in the jurisdiction of a signatory or the Government which has designated that signatory, provided that such use is necessary, and to the extent that it is necessary to use such inventions, technical data and information for the exercise of the right to use under paragraph (f) of this Article.

(h) The provisions of this Article shall not be held to apply to contracts for design, development, construction and establishment of the space segment to which the Corporation is a party on the date when the Agreement is first opened for signature. Subject to the provisions of Article 4 (c) of this Agreement, all such contracts shall be recognized by the Committee as continuing obligations for budgetary purposes.

Article 11

Each signatory shall keep such books, records, vouchers and accounts of all costs for which it is authorized to be reimbursed under this Special Agreement with respect to the design, development, construction, establishment, maintenance and operation of the space segment as may be appropriate and shall at all reasonable times make them available for inspection by members of the Committee.

Article 12

In addition to functions stated elsewhere in this Special Agreement, the Corporation, as manager pursuant to Article VIII of the Agreement, shall:

(a) prepare and submit to the Committee the annual programs and budgets;

(b) recommend to the Committee the type or types of space segment to be established;

(c) plan, conduct, arrange for and co-operate in studies, design work and development for improvement of the space segment;

(d) operate and maintain the space segment;

(e) furnish to the Committee such information as may be required by any representative on the Committee to enable him to discharge his responsibilities as a representative;

(f) arrange for technicians, selected by the Committee with the concurrence of the Corporation from among persons nominated by signatories, to participate in the assessment of designs and of specifications for equipment for the space segment;

(g) use its best efforts to arrange for inventions, technical data and information arising directly from any jointly financed work performed under contracts placed before the date on which the Agreement is opened for signature to be disclosed to each signatory and to be made available for use free of charge in the design, development, manufacture and use of equipment and components for the space segment by each signatory or any person in the jurisdiction of the signatory or the Government which has designated that signatory.

Article 13

Neither the Corporation as signatory or manager, nor any other signatory as such shall be liable to any other signatory for loss or damage sustained by reason of a failure or breakdown of a satellite at or after launching or a failure or breakdown of any other portion of the space segment.

Article 14

Arrangements shall be made whereby all legal disputes arising in connection with this Special Agreement or in connection with the rights and obligations of signatories can, if not otherwise settled, be submitted to the decision of an impartial tribunal, to be established in accordance with such arrangements, which would decide such questions in accordance with general principles of law. To this end, a group of legal experts appointed by the signatories and by the prospective signatories listed in the Annex to this Agreement when it is first opened for signature shall recommend a draft of a Supplementary Agreement containing such arrangements; the signatories shall, after considering that draft, conclude a Supplementary Agreement for such arrangements within a period of three months from the date when the Agreement is first opened for signature. The Supplementary Agreement shall be binding on all those who subsequently become signatories to this Special Agreement.

Article 15

Any proposed amendment to this Special Agreement shall first be submitted to the Committee. If recommended by the Committee for adoption, it shall enter into force for all signatories when notifications of approval have been deposited with the Government of the United States of America by two-thirds of the signatories, provided that no amendment may impose upon any signatory any additional financial obligation without its consent.

Article 16

This Special Agreement shall enter into force for each signatory on the day of signature, provided that the Agreement shall have entered into force for or shall have been provisionally applied by the Government which is or has designated the signatory in question; it shall continue in force for as long as the Agreement continues in force.

DONE at Washington this twentieth day of August 1964, in the English and French languages, both texts being equally authoritative, in a single original, which shall be deposited in the archives of the Government of the United States of America, which shall transmit a certified copy to each signatory or acceding Government and to the Government of each State which is a member cf the International Telecommunication Union.

ON ARBITRATION

(a) *Status of the Agreement*

Enters into force when it has been signed by all signatories to the Special Agreement in respect of which the Special Agreement is in force.

As of 31 December 1965 the following States were parties to this agreement: Argentina (7/6/65),[1] Australia (4/6/65), Austria (8/6/65), Belgium (4/6/65), Canada (4/6/65), Ceylon (7/6/65), China (4/6/65), Colombia (4/6/65), Denmark (4/6/65), Ethiopia (10/6/65), France (4/6/65), Germany (Fed. Rep.) (4/6/65), Greece (9/6/65), India (30/8/65), Indonesia (4/6/65), Iraq (27/10/65), Ireland (4/6/65), Israel (4/6/65), Italy (4/6/65), Japan (4/6/65), Jordan (22/6/65), Lebanon (4/6/65), Libya (4/6/65), Monaco (7/4/65), The Netherlands (4/6/65), New Zealand (9/6/65), Norway (7/6/65), Pakistan (10/9/65), Portugal (4/6/65), Saudi Arabia (1/9/65), South Africa (15/6/65), Spain (4/6/65), Sweden (4/6/65), Switzerland (4/6/65), United Arab Republic (4/6/65), United Kingdom (4/6/65), United States of America (4/6/65), Vatican City (16/6/65), Yemen (29/6/65).

(b) *Text of the Agreement*

Whereas Article 14 of the Special Agreement signed pursuant to Article II of the Agreement Establishing Interim Arrangements for a Global Commercial Communications Satellite System opened for signature on 20 August 1964, at Washington provides for arrangements to be made by a Supplementary Agreement whereby legal disputes may, if not otherwise settled, be submitted to the decision of an impartial tribunal;

It is hereby agreed as follows:

Article 1

In this Supplementary Agreement:

(a) 'The Agreement' means the Agreement Establishing Interim Arrangements for a Global Commercial Communications Satellite System opened for signature on 20 August 1964, at Washington;

(b) 'The Special Agreement' means the Special Agreement signed pursuant to Article II of the Agreement;

(c) 'The Committee' means the Interim Communications Satellite Committee established by Article IV of the Agreement;

(d) 'Signatory' means, as in the Special Agreement, a Government or communications entity which has signed the Special Agreement and in respect of which it is in force.

Article 2

(a) An arbitral tribunal constituted under this Supplementary Agreement is competent to give a decision in any legal dispute over the following

[1] Figure shown in brackets is date of signature. The list appears in the *Yearbook of Air and Space Law 1965*, p. 436.

matter: whether an action or a failure to act by the Committee or by any signatory or signatories is authorized by or is in compliance with the Agreement and the Special Agreement.

(b) An arbitral tribunal constituted in accordance with this Supplementary Agreement shall also be competent to give a decision on any legal dispute arising in connection with any other agreement relating to the arrangements established by the Agreement and the Special Agreement where the signatories which are parties to that other agreement have agreed to confer such a competence. A tribunal in exercising such competence shall act in accordance with the agreement which confers competence on it.

(c) Only the following may be parties in arbitration proceedings instituted under this Supplementary Agreement:

(i) Any signatory,
(ii) The Committee.

Article 3

(a) Within 30 days of the entry into force of this Supplementary Agreement and every two years thereafter, each signatory shall submit to the Committee the name of a legal expert of generally recognized ability who will be available for the succeeding two years to serve as president of tribunals constituted under this Supplementary Agreement. From such nominees the Committee shall appoint seven individuals to a panel from which presidents of tribunals shall be selected.

(b) The members of the panel shall be appointed by the unanimous agreement of the members of the Committee or, if not so appointed within three months from the entry into force of this Supplementary Agreement and every two years thereafter, by a decision of the Committee taken in the same manner mentioned in Article v (c) of the Agreement in respect of the matters listed in sub-paragraphs (i) to (xiv) of that paragraph. The members of the panel shall be:[1]

[1] For the list of States parties to the main Agreement (48 at the end of 1965), and of the States and organizations parties to the special Agreement, see *Yearbook of Air and Space Law 1965*, p. 422. Both Agreements entered into force on 20 August 1964.

Appendix VI

OUTER SPACE TREATY 1966[1]

Preamble

The States parties to this treaty,

Inspired by the great prospects opening up before mankind as a result of man's entry into outer space;

Recognizing the common interest of all mankind in the progress of the exploration and use of outer space for peaceful purposes;

Believing that the exploration and use of outer space should be carried on for the benefit of all peoples irrespective of the degree of their economic or scientific development;

Desiring to contribute to broad international co-operation in the scientific as well as the legal aspects of the exploration and use of outer space for peaceful purposes;

Believing that such co-operation will contribute to the development of mutual understanding and to the strengthening of friendly relations between States and peoples;

Recalling [the] Resolution entitled 'Declaration of Legal Principles Governing the Activities of States in the Exploration and Use of Outer Space', which was adopted unanimously by the U.N. General Assembly on 13 December 1963;

Recalling [the] Resolution calling upon States to refrain from placing in orbit around the earth any objects carrying nuclear weapons or any other kinds of weapons of mass destruction or from installing such weapons on celestial bodies, which was adopted unanimously by the U.N. General Assembly on 17 October 1963.

Taking account of [the] U.N. General Assembly Resolution of 3 November 1947, which condemned propaganda designed or likely to provoke or encourage any threat to the peace, breach of the peace, or act of aggression and considering that the aforementioned resolution is applicable to outer space;

Convinced that a treaty on principles governing the activities of States in the exploration and use of outer space, including the moon and other celestial bodies, will further the purposes and principles of the Charter of the United Nations;

Have agreed on the following:

Article 1

The exploration and use of outer space, including the moon and other celestial bodies, shall be carried out for the benefit and in the interests of all countries, irrespective of their degree of economic or scientific development, and shall be the province of all mankind.

[1] Entered into force 10 October 1967, 16 countries then being parties, including the U.S.A., U.S.S.R. and U.K. France has signed but not ratified. China is not a party.

Outer space, including the moon and other celestial bodies, shall be free for exploration and use by all States without discrimination of any kind, on a basis of equality and in accordance with international law, and there shall be free access to all areas of celestial bodies.

There shall be freedom of scientific investigation in outer space, including the moon and other celestial bodies, and States shall facilitate and encourage international co-operation in such investigation.

Article 2

Outer space, including the moon and other celestial bodies, is not subject to national appropriation by claim of sovereignty, by means of use or occupation, or by any other means.

Article 3

States parties to the treaty shall carry on activities in the exploration and use of outer space, including the moon and other celestial bodies, in accordance with international law, including the Charter of the United Nations, in the interest of maintaining international peace and security and promoting international co-operation and understanding.

Article 4

States parties to the treaty undertake not to place in orbit around the earth any objects carrying nuclear weapons or any other kinds of weapons of mass destruction, install such weapons on celestial bodies, or station such weapons in outer space in any other manner.

The moon and other celestial bodies shall be used by all States parties to the treaty exclusively for peaceful purposes. The establishment of military bases, installations, and fortifications, the testing of any type of weapons, and the conduct of military manœuvres on celestial bodies shall be forbidden. The use of military personnel for scientific research or for any other peaceful purposes shall not be prohibited. The use of any equipment or facility necessary for peaceful exploration of the moon and other celestial bodies shall also not be prohibited.

Article 5

States parties to the treaty shall regard astronauts as envoys of mankind in outer space and shall render to them all possible assistance in the event of accident, distress, or emergency landing on the territory of another State party or on the high seas. When astronauts make such a landing, they shall be safely and promptly returned to the State of registry of their space vehicle.

In carrying on activities in outer space and on celestial bodies, the astronauts of one State party shall render all possible assistance to the astronauts of other States parties.

States parties to the treaty shall immediately inform the other States parties to the treaty or the Secretary-General of the United Nations of any phenomena they discover in outer space, including the moon and other celestial bodies, which could constitute a danger to the life or health of astronauts.

Article 6

States parties to the treaty shall bear international responsibility for national activities in outer space, including the moon and other celestial bodies, whether such activities are carried on by governmental agencies or by non-governmental entities, and for assuring that national activities are carried out in conformity with the provisions set forth in the present treaty.

The activities of non-governmental entities in outer space, including the moon and other celestial bodies, shall require authorization and continuing supervision by the State concerned. When activities are carried on in outer space, including the moon and other celestial bodies, by an international organization, responsibility for compliance with this treaty shall be borne both by the international organization and by the States parties to the treaty participating in such organization.

Article 7

Each State party to the treaty that launches or procures the launching of an object into outer space, including the moon and other celestial bodies, and each State party from whose territory or facility an object is launched, is internationally liable for damage to another State party to the treaty or to its natural or juridical persons by such object or its component parts on the earth, in airspace, or in outer space, including the moon and other celestial bodies.

Article 8

A State party to the treaty on whose registry an object launched into outer space is carried shall retain jurisdiction and control over such object, and over any personnel thereof, while in outer space or on a celestial body. Ownership of objects launched into outer space, including objects landed or constructed on a celestial body, and of their component parts, is not affected by their presence in outer space, including the body, or by their return to the earth. Such objects or component parts found beyond the limits of the State party to the treaty on whose registry they are carried shall be returned to that State, which shall, upon request, furnish identifying data prior to their return.

Article 9

In the exploration and use of outer space, including the moon and other celestial bodies, States parties to the treaty shall be guided by the principle of co-operation and mutual assistance and shall conduct all their activities in outer space, including the moon and other celestial bodies, with due regard to the corresponding interests of all other States parties to the treaty.

States parties to the treaty shall pursue studies of outer space, including the moon and other celestial bodies, and conduct exploration of them so as to avoid their harmful contamination and also adverse changes in the environment of the Earth resulting from the introduction of extraterrestrial matter, and, where necessary, shall adopt appropriate measures for this purpose.

If a State party to the treaty has reason to believe that an activity or experiment planned by it or its nationals in outer space, including the moon and other celestial bodies, would cause potentially harmful interference with activities of other States parties in the peaceful exploration and use of outer space, including the moon and other celestial bodies, it shall undertake appropriate international consultations before proceeding with any such activity or experiment.

A State party to the treaty which has reason to believe that an activity or experiment planned by another State party in outer space, including the moon and other celestial bodies, would cause potentially harmful interference with activities in the peaceful exploration and use of outer space, including the moon and other celestial bodies, may request consultation concerning the activity or experiment.

Article 10

In order to promote international co-operation in the exploration and use of outer space, including the moon and other celestial bodies, in conformity with the purposes of this treaty, the States parties to the treaty shall consider on a basis of equality any requests by other States parties to the treaty to be afforded an opportunity to observe the flight of space objects launched by those States. The nature of such an opportunity for observation and the conditions under which it could be afforded shall be determined by agreement between the States concerned.

Article 11

In order to promote international co-operation in the peaceful exploration and use of outer space, States parties to the treaty conducting activities in outer space, including the moon and other celestial bodies, agree to inform the Secretary-General of the United Nations as well as the public and the international scientific community, to the greatest extent feasible and practicable, of the nature, conduct, locations, and results of such activities. On receiving the said information, the U.N. Secretary-General should be prepared to disseminate it immediately and effectively.

Article 12

All stations, installations, equipment, and space vehicles on the moon and other celestial bodies shall be open to representatives of other States parties to the treaty, on a basis of reciprocity. Such representatives shall give reasonable advance notice of a projected visit, in order that appropriate consultations may be held and that maximum precautions may be taken to assure safety and to avoid interference with normal operations in the facility to be visited.

Article 13

The provisions of this treaty shall apply to the activities of States parties to the treaty in the exploration and use of outer space, including the moon and other celestial bodies, whether such activities are carried on by a single State party to the treaty or jointly with other States, including cases where they are carried on within the framework of international inter-governmental organizations.

Any practical questions arising in connexion with activities carried on by international inter-governmental organizations in the exploration and use of outer space, including the moon and other celestial bodies, shall be resolved by the States parties to the treaty either with the appropriate international organization or with one or more State members of that international organization, which are parties to this treaty.

Article 14

(1) This treaty shall be open to all States for signature. Any State which does not sign this treaty before its entry into force in accordance with Paragraph 3 of this Article may accede to it at any time.

(2) This treaty shall be subject to ratification by signatory States. Instruments of ratification and of accession shall be deposited with the Governments of the Union of Soviet Socialist Republics, the United Kingdom of Great Britain and Northern Ireland, and the United States of America, which are hereby designated the Depositary Governments.

(3) This treaty shall enter into force upon the deposit of instruments of ratification by five Governments, including the Governments designated as Depositary Governments.

(4) For States whose instruments of ratification or accession are deposited subsequent to the entry into force of this treaty, it shall enter into force on the date of the deposit of their instruments of ratification or accession.

(5) The Depositary Governments shall promptly inform all signatory and acceding States of the date of each signature, the date of deposit of each instrument of ratification of and accession to this treaty, the date of its entry into force, and other notices.

(6) This treaty shall be registered by the Depositary Governments pursuant to Article 102 of the U.N. Charter.

Article 15

Any State party to the treaty may propose amendments to this treaty. Amendments shall enter into force for each State party to the treaty accepting the amendments upon their acceptance by a majority of the States parties to the treaty, and thereafter for each remaining State party to the treaty on the date of acceptance by it.

Article 16

Any State party to the treaty may give notice of its withdrawal from the treaty one year after its entry into force by written notification to the Depositary Governments. Such withdrawal shall take effect one year from the date of receipt of this notification.

Article 17

This treaty of which the Chinese, English, French, Russian, and Spanish texts are equally authentic, shall be deposited in the archives of the Depositary Governments. Duly certified copies . . . shall be transmitted to the Governments of the signatory and acceding States.

INDEX